It's That Simple!

A Man's Book on Relationships, Life, Ourselves
and The Healing of it All

Bree Maresca-Kramer M.A.

It's
That
Simple!

Published and Distributed by: It's That Simple!

Editorial Services by: Zuula Consulting LLC

Design Services by: SWD7 Mike Novick

This book is not intended to take the place of medical or psychological diagnosis, treatment, or advice from a trained professional. Readers are advised to consult a physician or other qualified health professionals regarding treatment of any medical or psychological problems. In the event that you use any of the information in this book for yourself, the author and publisher assume no responsibility for your actions.

Library of Congress Cataloging-in-Publication Data

ISBN 978-1-935658-01-6

Printed in the United States of America

"Guys, this book gets it right! Bree Maresca-Kramer understands women and she understands us too! You will love her direct and pragmatic wisdom. Instead of pounding us with rules, she enables us with tools. ***It's That Simple!*** is an outstanding easy to read book."

Dr. Jason P. Schwartz, Physician, Educator, Author

"Go ahead! Pick up this book and read it! You will find simple, honest, and easy to understand information, which allows every man to know how to participate in a loving relationship! Bree Maresca-Kramer teaches us to access our inner best to understand and love both our partner and ourselves."

Petrina McGowen, LMFT, Marriage and Family Therapist

"Wow! ***It's That Simple!*** is an amazing step-by step guide with nuanced ideas and creative paths to finding your own authentic life and powerful relationships. We highly recommend it!"

Donna Mahoney-Lynch, D Min, Pastoral Counseling, Author
Tim Mahoney-Lynch, MSW, Marriage and Family Counselor

"***It's That Simple!*** is remarkable! It provided me with so many answers about women and new insights about myself. This is a great must read book for all men who can't understand the women in their life!"

Terry G. Donaho, Firefighter/Paramedic

This book is dedicated to You.
May you discover your Most Precious Self
and then See the same in your partner.

And...

To My Beautiful Daughter,
Alexis-Briana Laura Kramer,
You light up my life and expand my heart
Each and every day with Great Joy and Love,
Just by being who you are...
I Love You for Eternity!

Acknowledgements

I would like to thank each of the wonderful souls who have assisted me along the way on my journey. I extend my warmest gratitude and love for all you have done in my life.

I would like to especially thank my Mom, Barbara, for being an amazing example of inner strength and perseverance, my Dad, Joe, for teaching me that when life hands you lemons you make lemonade, my family, my dearest friends who are my extended family, Gordon for the countless blessings his love and support have brought, and finally to all of my incredible clients whom over the years have allowed me the honor to travel with them on their most sacred journey into themselves.

Contents

Introduction

I once shared with a female friend, *If only women knew how easy it really is and how little it really takes for a man to be happy in a relationship*. She interjected sarcastically, "Oh really? Please fill me in because I can't figure these men out!" Right around that same time, a male friend asked for help with women. When I answered, *If men only knew how little it takes and how simple it is for a woman to blossom in his midst.* He interrupted and said, "What? Women and simple in the same sentence? I can't figure you women out!"

In each of these moments, I asked myself, *Where do I begin and how can I simply explain what I know will help?*

Providing the answers to these questions soon became a desire to help both men and women—and as many as I could.

As this desire grew, I noticed that out of nowhere, the individuals I was working with were encouraging me to, "Write all this stuff down Bree!" The inspiration from these friends and clients truly was the origin of this book—questions answered, which turned into a desire, which then turned into action.

So here we are now in this very moment, you and I, about to embark on this journey together. As you read this book, I hope you feel as if I am right there with you—sharing with you, offering guidance, and making available to you actual and practical tools that will help you.

My intention is to encourage you, support you, honor you on your own inner journey, and provide the tools you can use for yourself, your life, and your relationships—especially the one with your woman.

While you are reading, please be aware of the fact that I will be stating, sharing, and explaining my concepts, ideas, tools, and thought systems in a very over-generalized fashion. I am doing this so the information can be as straightforward, easy, and enjoyable as possible.

From my personal and professional experience, I have found that when we allow ourselves to lighten up and find the humor in our situations, all of the heavy and confusing aspects of our lives become much easier to handle. By keeping all of this information as enjoyable as possible, you will have the opportunity to figure out, face, and fix the parts that might otherwise be too much to deal with.

What I am sharing in this book has come not only from my educational and professional experience, but also "through" me from that which I call The Divine.

Therefore, as you read, I encourage you to simply take what you like and leave the rest.

If what you are reading rings true with you, it *is* for you. On the contrary, if it does not feel right, leave it and move on.

You are beginning the most important journey you can ever take…the journey into You.

1

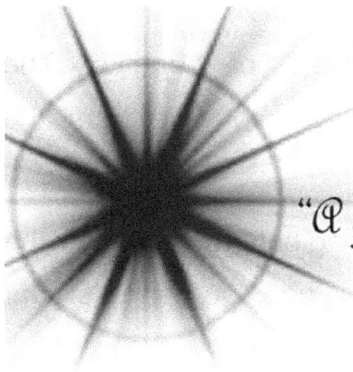

GETTING STARTED

"A journey of a thousand miles must begin with a single step."

Lao Tzu, founder of Taoism (600 BC – 531 BC)

Welcome to the first step.

To get you started, you will be creating your own personal toolbox. Actually building one is not necessary, for you are going to use your imagination. You can make your toolbox look any way you would like. The only requirement is that it is strong, sturdy, and dependable.

Ready? Okay, here we go...using your most vivid imagination, close your eyes, and create a toolbox in your mind.

Do you have your toolbox in your mind?

Great!

You will receive the "tools" to fill it as you continue reading.

These tools are very practical.

They provide layers upon layers of benefits. The wonderful part about them is that the more you use them, the more benefits you will receive.

Since, this toolbox is in your imagination, you have the power to take it with you anywhere you go. You can use your tools anytime and in any place you would like.

By taking your tools and applying them as needed, you will have the opportunity to experience remarkable transformations in yourself, your life, and your relationships.

The first tool to put in your toolbox is a simple one.

It is a personal notebook.

This notebook can be any kind you would like to have. It can be a spiral-bound one children use in school or a grand professional leather-bound one.

The primary purpose of your personal notebook is to have it ready as a place in which you will be able to: take notes, provide answers to questions you will be reading, journal in, draw in, and assist in your process. I use this tool with everyone I work with and although very simple, it consistently works wonders!

Now we are ready.

You have your personal toolbox and notebook.

We are going to start from a common ground of understanding. This ground has to do with all of us: men and women.

You see, men and women are "wired" differently.

What I mean by this is—for the most part—men and women think, feel, experience, communicate, and understand life differently.

Men are not better than women; nor are women better than men.

We are just different.

Each gender has its own strengths and areas that need some assistance. It is very easy to breeze by this fact as just another common cliché and say something like, "Yeah...Yeah...Yeah...men and women are different—big deal!" However, fully acknowledging this concept helps us all gain a deeper understanding of the opposite sex and ourselves.

Simply put, on a physical human level, the women in your life—your wife, girlfriend, lover, friend, mother, sister, aunt, daughter, boss, friend, etc., are different from you.

They do not feel, understand, or communicate like you.

Men are not like women.

Women are not like men.

I am stressing this fact because truly understanding the difference between men and women is the foundation from which we all need to start.

Once we have this understanding, we all are able to treat one another with compassion, empathy, respect, and great unconditional love. Coming from such a place is the springboard for all healthy relationships.

Ultimately, every one of us—men, women, and children—all want the same thing. We all want to be seen (validated), heard (listened to), and loved for exactly who we are—"warts" and all. We all want our loved ones and the world around us to recognize our brilliance and appreciate how awesome we are, while downplaying our "warts." In short, we all yearn for complete acceptance and unconditional love.

However, when you take a long and honest look at most relationships, usually and ironically, what we all want—unconditional love and acceptance—we end up withholding not only from ourselves but from one another as well. Why do we do this?

For the most part, I believe we do this out of lack of knowledge and awareness. In other words, we are not aware that we are withholding these things and just do not know how to do it any better.

I truly believe most people do the best they can.

What I mean is that most people are operating in their lives at their current place of knowledge and understanding. Therefore, when people are unaware of something, such as an issue they may have, or a dysfunctional behavioral pattern they exhibit, they simply cannot do it differently. When people gain insight and self-awareness, they, then, become able to make changes in the way they treat others and themselves.

The key here is that individuals must gain SELF-awareness and insight. People do not "get it" just because they are told, even if they are told by a therapist. It is not until the person is ready that they will understand. Therefore, a wife telling her husband that he has intimacy problems will never work.

We all must come to our own "Ah-ha!" moment and then desire to gain the knowledge needed for healing the wounded places within.

2

BEING THE ARTIST OF YOU

"It's on the strength of observation and reflection that one finds a way. So we must dig and delve unceasingly."

Claude Monet, French Impressionist (1840 – 1926)

In this exact moment, the man you are is a culmination of all the experiences in your life. You are now a direct result of exactly how you perceived and came away from all of your life experiences—from birth to this present moment.

In other words, you are the painting of your own life.

If you could look in the mirror right now, what type of painting would you see? What does your self-portrait look like? What colors, shades, and hues show up and what do they represent in your painting? What type of textures, light effects, and brush strokes make up your painting?

Now looking at your self-portrait, say to yourself:

I am the artist of this painting. I have created this all by myself.

The common response to this statement is often,
"No way! He did this...she did that to me...my childhood was

awful...my wife is always nagging at me...and my boss doesn't respect me!" On and on it can go. However, the truth is you are the artist of your portrait.

No one else.

Here is an example to help make more sense out of what I am talking about. Let us say, that during your childhood you were raised by a raging alcoholic who beat you. Although abuse is extremely difficult, how this abuse affects your life and your self-portrait is still up to you.

You could take away from this abuse, life is hard, people are not to be trusted, and I am never safe. In this case, your portrait could look dark, bitter, sour, frightening, and angry. With the canvas covered in resentment, this portrait would be painted with a victim mentality.

On the other hand, you could walk away from this childhood with gratitude. This gratitude could come from a place of understanding that *precisely* because of your raging alcoholic parent you are now a richer, deeper, more compassionate human being with the ability to see past an addiction into the heart of someone and the greater purpose of life. In this case, your portrait could be a beautiful one, filled with brightness, light, hope, innocence, forgiveness, understanding, and love.

See?

How you paint your portrait is all in your perception. It is all in how you interpret the situation. Your interpretation—and thus your thinking about it—creates your self-portrait. You, your perceptions, and your thoughts create everything. You create the colors, lighting, texture, brush strokes, and the overall feel of the portrait.

You are the sole artist of you!

So, how does being the artist apply to your relationship with yourself and your woman? Well, let us say your portrait is more of a collage. There are places where it is very polished, bright, magnificent, and other places that are abstract, dark, sad, lonely, and scary. Most of the time, when we first meet a potential mate, we show the "good" parts of our portrait. We proudly show all of the impressive colors, textures, lighting effects, and overall brilliance of who we are, right? Come on. You know it's true. We all do it! Then, later down the road of your relationship, these "other parts" of your portrait start seeping through. You try not to let the negative features reveal themselves, but after all, it is your portrait. How could every detail not eventually be shown?

Reaching this point in a relationship is generally when you will hear men say something like, "She is not who I thought she was. She turned out to be crazy, just like the rest of them. I can never find the right woman." This is also the time when you will see people run away from the relationship, or at least want to.

Here are men and women, very different creatures, doing the very same thing. We are each trying to hide the parts of our portraits that we believe are not attractive. To add to this, we each secretly or unconsciously expect the other to "fix" or make beautiful those "dark" or "ugly" parts we created in our self-portrait. Now, I say *secretly* or *unconsciously* because most of us do not walk around consciously holding up our self-portraits, announcing to the world that these difficult parts of our portrait need to be fixed by our partner or the relationship. However, if we are really honest with one another and ourselves, most of the time, we find precisely this situation.

Can you imagine how futile this is?

Here we all are, walking around life displaying our self-portraits and proclaiming the "wrong" or "bad" parts—which we painted ourselves—must be corrected by another. When you think about, it is absolutely absurd and hilarious.

However, when starting a relationship, more often than not it is as if we bump into one another and unconsciously utter to ourselves, *Hmmmm, maybe, just maybe this person will make it all better.* Consequently, we frequently enter a relationship from a place of perceived lack instead of a place of wholeness. This place of perceived lack, then leads to behaviors that occur simply to try to get the "bad" parts of our portrait repainted by our partner. These behaviors are exhibited through different forms of manipulation, guilt, and control. Ironically, these are the precise behaviors that are normally labeled "bad" or "ugly." Yet, these are the ones that eventually show up in our relationships.

Let us dive into this concept a bit further with a common example. Say one of the "bad" parts of someone's portrait is having low self-esteem. This part then drives the person to create circumstances and situations in order to be "fed," "affirmed," and "recognized" by the other person. In other words, they seek to have their lack of a healthy and positive self-image fixed by the other person. Paradoxically, it is impossible for a person to fix another person. For example, a woman with low self-esteem can be told a hundred times a day how wonderful, beautiful, smart, and amazing she is; however, it will not change how she truly feels about herself inside. She is the only one who can change this.

When learning this pattern of expecting the other person to paint the "ugly" parts of our portrait away, it is especially easy to think, "Oh, not me, I don't act like that. I'm not asking my partner to fix me." If this sounds familiar, I challenge you to do one thing: I challenge you to employ the tools I like to call, ***being consciously aware*** and ***acting as the objective observer of You***. These simple tools have the potential to provide incredible healing for yourself and your relationships.

Therefore, it is essential you understand exactly what these terms entail.

Consciousness can be divided into three parts: the conscious mind, subconscious mind, and unconscious mind. The unconscious mind is where everything is stored. Like a constant video recorder, it is always capturing, recording, and filing away every single moment and experience you have. The subconscious mind provides the ability to recall a past experience and then bring it to the awareness of the conscious mind. The conscious mind is aware of what is happening in this very moment—in this *now* moment.

Let me ask you, what are you aware of in this exact moment? Are you aware that you are reading? Are you aware of the words on the page or perhaps the type of paper the words are printed on? Are you aware of some body aches or pains you may be experiencing? Are you aware of the thoughts you are having? Simply put, in order to become consciously aware you must merely become aware of *you* in the present, *now* moment.

The next tool is to become the objective observer of you. I use the word "objective" because it denotes the absence of any judgment either good or bad. Being an objective observer is very important. The practice here is not to judge yourself, but simply to become consciously aware of yourself. This means you will become aware of your thoughts—either conscious or unconscious—your words, your intentions, your desires, your fears, your motives, and your actions.

Quite often, as we move through the day, we are running on an "autopilot" or "asleep" mode. It is as if we move through the day without being aware of what is actually occurring on a deeper, more meaningful level. A very common example of this state occurs when we pay for items at the grocery store. Most of the time the cashier and we (the consumer) mutually are not really connecting or interacting. Rather, we are merely going through the motions of this activity. Being in this "autopilot" or "asleep" state often leaves us acting, reacting, and living from an uninformed and mechanical state of mind.

Albert Einstein once said, "Insanity is doing the same thing over and over again and expecting different results." In order to avoid this type of "insanity," we must first become aware of those aspects we continue repeating. Employing the tools of being consciously aware and acting as the objective observer will allow you the opportunity to obtain the required information for making positive changes within yourself and your relationships.

Okay, here is how it works:

Being consciously aware and acting as the objective observer of you is simply consciously stepping outside yourself and observing. Have you ever seen a movie, read a book, or watched a television program in which the main character was also the narrator? Well, that element is close to what I am talking about here. Every day, you make a conscious decision to wake up, step outside of the "autopilot" you, watch, and learn all about you. This process can actually become quite enlightening and humorous once you get the hang of it.

As you are doing this, I want you to simply say to yourself after each observation, *Hmmm, Isn't that interesting?* Using this phrase will help you avoid the pitfall of judging your observations as either good or bad. Instead, you will be learning how to neutralize the observations of any emotionally charged reaction, so you are able to extract valuable information.

Okay, it is time to put this into practice.

In this very moment, close your eyes, and simply observe.

Observe You.

Observe your thoughts.

Observe your feelings.

Observe your body.

Observe all of You.

Did you go blank? Did you have a hard time coming up with anything? Maybe it felt ridiculous or uncomfortable for you. Perhaps, it felt as if you cannot do this. Could it be you were trying too hard to observe? Do not worry—all of these experiences are normal in the beginning!

Now, to practice again, continue reading. As you are reading these words, printed on this paper, I would like you to simply observe any thoughts floating across your mind. The words on this paper are just that—words on paper. Notice what is coming to mind. The font size, type, and color are all in front of you on this paper. Your eyes are passing over each word. Your mind is processing what it is reading according to your experiences. What thoughts are happening now? Your feelings about what you are reading have nothing to do with the words on this page. The actual words you are reading are emotionally neutral, printed letters on a piece of paper. Your interpretation of these words is the important part. How do these words stir you? Are you getting annoyed? Does this seem monotonous or brainless? Continue reading the words on this page as if you were just the radio announcer at a baseball game. Simply report to the crowd what the player (you) is doing. The words will continue one after another and another. Each word will follow another and then another until you finish reading this book. What are you thinking about right now?

Learning how to become consciously aware and the objective observer of you, is a very simple technique. However, it is not necessarily easy in the beginning. If this exercise were difficult for you, that is normal. It does get easier. As with any new concept or activity, you must expect a learning curve. Any new type of learning requires us to climb over a steep mountain. Once we reach the top of the learning mountain, the newly acquired information is then more readily understood and applied.

Being consciously aware and acting as the objective observer of you will get easier as you go along. Eventually it will become second nature to you. Soon, no matter what you are doing—reading, speaking, listening, working, or just being—you will be able to live consciously aware and act as the objective observer of You!

Are you having fun yet?

Diving into You is an excellent experience. The action of this is not always easy and takes a great deal of courage. Our lives are much easier when we stay on autopilot, because that takes very little effort. On the other hand, "diving deep" into oneself requires not only effort, but also a real depth of character. "Diving deep" means taking off the blinders, removing the barriers of self-deception and self-defense, and authentically looking at—and embracing—all of ourselves. Embracing all parts of yourself does not mean you will necessarily like all the present parts of you. It does mean, however, that you will be able to accept all the parts: the ones that feel good and the ones that do not feel so good.

This "deep diving" is a sure way to lead you to the most important human relationship you will ever have: the relationship with yourself. When we are in a loving and healthy place with ourselves, the world around us appears as a completely new painting. The canvas of this new world is unveiled as our mind's understanding and perception changes. A loving and healthy relationship with yourself is the cornerstone of a rich, happy, and fulfilling life—demonstrating itself in all of your experiences. From this place, you are able to co-create a rich and meaningful life. Your life can be experienced with all of your favorite colors, scenes, and special effects. You will have the ability to feel and experience abundance in all areas of your life. You will find that **You have the choice** to enjoy rather than endure. I am not saying there will never be times of challenge. However, because of your inner work, the challenging times can be viewed as opportunities, rather than moments of crisis and despair.

Sounds good doesn't it?

You can have it!

It really is all up to You.

Have you ever known someone in your life who is a truly happy person? Not that he or she doesn't have bad days now and then, but is genuinely happy? Think about it for a while. Most of the time, when I pose this question to my clients, they have a hard time naming someone specific. They might say something like, "I know what you mean." Then, when I ask if they know a sad or angry person, the client almost always has an individual more readily in mind.

> Do you know someone who is truly happy, sad, or angry?
>
> What do you think differentiates these individuals?
>
> How can someone be so happy and someone else so sad or angry?

I believe that everyone, no matter who they are and what they have been through, is basically dealing with the same issues. These issues can manifest in different forms and in varying degrees and layers. However, if we look closely, we can see that our individual issues are all fundamentally the same. I believe that when you break down all of the various issues people are dealing with, excluding any mental health disorders (such as chemical depression, bi-polar disorder, addictions, or psychosis), the core of human emotional unrest lies in the individual's perception.

So, in your opinion, what makes one person happy and another sad?

In this next exercise, I will use a hypothetical scene to further explain how perception affects us all:

First, we have person A, who is walking down the beach. Let us call him Joe. While Joe is taking his walk, he notices how amazing the water looks in brilliant shades of blue, green, and teal. He sees the sunlight moving across the remarkable colors of the water. He feels the sun warm his skin and body. The sand beneath his toes feels good as he walks. Joe smiles as he strolls down the beach, really enjoying this time to himself. As this is happening, Joe trips over a conch shell and cuts his toe. He stops in surprise then laughs when he turns around to see what he has tripped over. He picks up the shell and holds it to his ear, listening for the sound of the ocean. Pleased with his new discovery, he keeps the shell, washes off his cut toe in the lapping waves, and continues on his walk feeling good.

Now, let us look at the experience of person B, whom we will call James.

James is also walking down the beach enjoying the water, sand, sun, and is having an experience very similar to Joe's experience. While enjoying his time alone at the ocean, James also trips on the conch shell and cuts his toe. However, instead of finding the shell as a great discovery, James thinks to himself, "See? I can never have a good time. It's always something! Stupid shell. Why don't they clean up these beaches? Sure, they tax us until we can hardly afford anything and then blow it on nothing! They should be cleaning up these beaches, so people like me don't get hurt. Oh great! I'm bleeding! It might get infected. Stupid shell. Now I have to go home and put some antibacterial ointment on that cut. I can't even enjoy a little walk. Every time I start to have a little enjoyment, it is ruined! Why me, God? Why do these things always happen to me!?"

Quite a difference, wouldn't you say?

As you read James' thoughts as they are strung together, what do you gather from them?

James and Joe's experiences were polar opposites. Each person's perception was completely different. Same setting, beach, temperature, color of the water, etc. The only difference was their response. Joe perceived or interpreted the conch shell as a treasure. He placed a value on it, which enhanced his walking experience. He had very little reaction to his cut toe. In fact, Joe handled the accident as an insignificant part of his experience. James, on the other hand, perceived the conch shell as **the** negative reason his nice walk was ruined. From this perception, many of his negative belief systems were funneled out and exposed. Did James pay attention to this? Did he even realize all this negativity was inside him? Probably not.

If James had employed the technique of being consciously aware and acting as the objective observer, he would have had the opportunity to identify the following eight negative statements:

1. See? **I can never have a good time**.
2. **It's always something!** Stupid shell, why don't they clean up these beaches.
3. Sure, they tax us until **we can hardly afford anything** and then blow it on nothing!
4. They should be cleaning up these beaches, so **people like me** don't get hurt.
5. Oh great! I'm bleeding**, it might get infected**. Stupid shell. Now I have to go home and put some antibacterial ointment on that cut.
6. **I can't even enjoy a little walk.**
7. **Every time I start to have a little enjoyment, it is ruined**! Why me God?
8. Why do **these things always happen to me**?!

Upon recognizing his negative statements, James would have the opportunity to look at and piece together all his reactions—thus creating a "picture" of what is really going on inside his thought system.

These thoughts may be in James' conscious mind swirling around or they may actually be located in his unconscious mind. No matter the location of these thoughts, in order for James to experience changes in his life, he must identify and then change these thoughts into positive ones.

Harboring negative thoughts or viewpoints will eventually turn into a belief system. Whatever your belief system is will lead and dictate the direction and experiences of your life. This is why it is so important to identify what you are actually thinking and believing.

This concept of being consciously aware and acting as the objective observer often elicits a frustrated response from my clients. They tend to ask the same thing in a tone of utter disgust, "Bree, how do you expect me to walk around and stay consciously aware and be the objective observer all the time? It is too much work and I can't do it!"

You may be thinking the same thing at this moment, as well.

In the beginning, this technique can feel and seem overwhelming. To make it easier, really focus your attention on those times when you are feeling upset. Most often, when people are learning these tools, they have an easier time applying them when they are feeling upset.

The range of these upset emotions can be anywhere from a simple little annoyance to a full-blown anger. When you experience any type of these upset feelings, you can quickly spotlight detrimental thoughts representing your belief system. Once you start purposefully paying attention to your thoughts and reactions, you will be incredibly surprised at what you find!

Along the way, to receive all the benefits from applying these tools, remember to keep your personal notebook handy in order to jot down what you discover. Try to pay attention to any negative thoughts or beliefs you become aware of. Please remember that when you do this exercise, you are in a non-judgment zone. If what you are recognizing sounds "bad" to you, just respond with, *Hmmmm, Isn't that interesting? I didn't know that was in there. I am grateful to have this information.*

To get you started with using these tools, take the next few hours off from reading and concentrate on putting them to use. Focus on your everyday life and apply the tools as you see fit.

After the initial try with these tools, you will probably have gained some very valuable information about what is going on within you.

The more you actively employ your tools on a daily basis, the more your understanding will increase. The knowledge you will gain with these tools is necessary to move on to the next step and next tool.

If you do not feel you have a handle on this, please take your time and continue practicing being consciously aware and acting as the objective observer of you. When doing this, it is more important that you successfully get this step, rather than rushing through it. The more you try, the easier it will become.

Have fun with this exercise, it truly is an inside scoop into yourself.

We will assume that you are more able to identify the negative and harmful thoughts and beliefs you are carrying around inside of you. You are now ready for the next step.

At this point in the process, you may be thinking that this

experience is too much or too challenging. The important thing to know is—**It is all worth it!**

In the end, you will have attained so much valuable information for yourself, which will help you and your relationships—especially the one with your woman. However, I would like to tell you that it could get worse before it gets better. The reason is that you will be bringing up, confronting, and shining the spotlight on those unhealed places within you that you have likely been unaware of or tried to avoid. For most of us, this type of discovery is not comfortable or very easy.

The journey into self-awareness is not for the weak. However, if you honestly and bravely apply these tools and the ones you will learn as you continue reading, you will discover within yourself the inner courage, strength, and commitment to make it through to the other side. I promise you it is all worth it. On the other side of this journey is freedom! It is a place filled with self-honoring, joy, and a deeply meaningful and rich life. This freedom allows you the possibility to become a beacon that will inspire and teach others. You will stand as a testament that healing your life is possible. As well, your life can be a blessing to everyone around you. You will see and know it as you look into their eyes and observe their faces as they thank you for being who you are.

3

RE-SCRIPTING YOUR THOUGHTS

"Change your thoughts and you change your world."

Norman Vincent Peale, U.S. Clergyman, Author (1898 – 1993)

Now that you understand the idea of you being the artist of your portrait, it is time to step into the roles of writer, director, and producer of your thoughts and your life. You step into these roles by doing what I like to refer to as "re-scripting" your thoughts. When you re-script your thoughts, you are actually writing, directing, and producing a whole new life. Essentially, you will now be removing and re-writing the harmful thoughts and beliefs discovered by being consciously aware and acting as the objective observer of you. At first, this next step might feel contrived or fake and will probably be a bit uncomfortable. However, the more you do it, the more it will become a part of you. The real You.

Let us go back to James and his beach walking experience. If you recall, one of his negative messages was:

Every time I start to have a little enjoyment, it is ruined! When he recognizes this deeply held belief amidst his momentary frustration, James can say to himself, *Hmmmm, Isn't that interesting? I didn't know that thought was in there. I am so grateful to have this information.* From this point, he must move into consciously removing and re-scripting this thought. In order to do so, he can discover where this thought came from. He may determine this thought is not even his. Instead, perhaps it is one he repeatedly heard in childhood and then took on as his own. On the other hand, James may discover he adapted this belief after a series of events occurred in his life. He then internalized this belief as a concrete aspect of truth, which then directed his subsequent life experiences.

To start re-scripting your thoughts, begin by asking yourself, *Where is this thought coming from?* or *Whose thought is this?* Then, simply become still and allow the answer to be revealed to you. Remain still and listen. Asking these questions will most often elicit an image, a memory, or a sense of what the answer is.

Discovering where and how a thought came to be is not always necessary to remove and re-script it; however, sometimes it can make it easier.

Okay, back to James and his thought.

Let us say he figures out his thought, *Every time I start to have a little enjoyment, it is ruined!* originated in his childhood. He figures this out by asking himself, *Where did this thought come from?* Instantly, James gets an image from when he was eight-years old. He remembers his dad saying the very same thing to his mother. He further remembers that every time they went on any type of family outing, his dad would end up saying this because—for one reason or another—it would become true for him.

Immediately after these memories arise, James has an emotional response and becomes angry. He wants to blame his dad. He proclaims that because of his dad, he has been carrying around this thought inside of him all of these years. "He did this to me!" James thinks, only to continue the cyclical negative patterning of his life. However, being consciously aware and acting as an objective observer, this is the time to release the blame and start using his forgiveness paintbrush! This is where the process of re-scripting begins.

I believe the power of understanding provides the easiest route to forgiveness, no matter the circumstances. Once we understand, forgiveness is usually inevitable. In my professional and personal experience, I have only come across a few individuals who actually intended harm to others or their children. These very few people were either severely addicted and under the influence of drugs/alcohol or were suffering from a mental health disorder. The majority of people never intend to hurt others or pass negative patterns onto their children. More often than not, people really are doing the best they can and would choose to do it better if they knew how. However, when we are not aware enough within ourselves, we can unknowingly hurt others and pass along our issues to our children. Many parents share with me, that as a child, they made a promise to themselves to never treat their family the same way their parents treated them. Yet, now that they have children of their own, they are repeating the same negative behavior. "Why am I doing this?" they ask.

I liken their repeated behavior to a link in a chain.

Each generation is but a link connected to the one before. The unhealed or damaged parts of the previous links are passed to the next link and so the process continues. The cyclical behavior only stops when someone finally wakes up and declares, *That Is Enough!* From here, they realize what is going on and make the needed changes. By doing so, this person stops passing on negative beliefs and patterns to loved ones. Instead, they start passing on healing, uplifting, and positive beliefs and patterns.

People who can do this are very brave, strong, and committed. They are brave, because during this change, they may end up taking some grief from individuals in their life for shaking up the apple cart. In the process of healing, confrontations may happen with those we love because change commonly triggers fear in people. Ironically, even when the change is positive, people can react negatively. They may rebel against the new way and want to hold on to the old, even if the past behavior is not working or is dysfunctional. This is the point at which staying strong and committed to breaking the negative cycle really comes into play.

It is so easy to conform. Breaking the negative patterns and behaviors of the past takes great courage and fortitude. It is easy to go back to sleep, staying unconscious, and living on autopilot.

It is easy not to upset the apple cart. However, when it comes to truly enjoying life, it is magnificent to wake up! We break freely away from harmful behaviors, heal, and live happily from a place of fulfillment, abundance, joy, purpose, and creation!

In order to break the heavy chains of a negative cycle:

Forgiveness through understanding.

Forgiveness through understanding.

Forgiveness through understanding.

Go ahead. Say it to yourself three times. Now, test yourself. Think about the last time you were incredibly angry with someone. Think of a time when you were so angry you were shaking. Can you remember? Now, how did you feel as they explained their side of the situation? Were you able to gain some understanding of their perspective? Did you feel your anger start to melt away while your body and emotions calmed down? Were you able to put yourself in their shoes and understand what they were talking about?

If you have had this experience, it is because you allowed yourself to "see" through the other person's "vision." Every aspect in your life is experienced through your own personal "vision." This "vision" comes from your human conditions—your personality type, your upbringing, your unmet childhood needs and/or desires, your thoughts, and your perceptions. I call this "vision" your filters. So, for example, when you are in a situation with someone with whom you feel angry, you are experiencing the circumstance through your own filters—just as they are experiencing the circumstance through their own filters. You see, in this type of situation everyone is right and everyone's feelings are valid, for each person is having the experience through their own filters. Through the power of understanding, our perception of a situation can change. Thus, our thoughts, beliefs, and feelings toward the experience can change.

Let's consider James again.

Imagine he finds it within himself to gain some understanding about his father. Perhaps he realizes his father never fulfilled his lifelong dream. Maybe in his childhood, his father never felt really loved and cared for by his parents. Possibly, his father felt as if he could never measure up to his perfect older brother. Whatever the reason, by working through his own negative reactions and exploring and gaining awareness, James is able to understand his father did not plan to cause him emotional harm. He realizes that in his own way, his father did love him. He understands that he did the best he could with what he was capable of giving. With that understanding, James' perception has changed.

Ah-ha! Now we have a breakthrough!

James has discovered where this thought originated, has worked through his emotional reaction of anger and blame, and has moved past the filter into understanding. Now, James is ready to permanently remove and re-script this thought!

I have used the following exercise specifically for removing unwanted, harmful, or negative thoughts with my clients, as well as in my own personal healing path. This tool works wonders. However, as they say in the twelve-step programs, "It works if you work it." Successful healing depends on the consistent and diligent implementation of your tools in your daily life. With dedication and commitment to your process, you will experience new and positive changes in your life.

To begin with this next exercise, read over all of the following four steps. Then reread each step one-by-one, giving individual attention to the guidance. Becoming familiar and comfortable with each step will allow you to put re-scripting into action both quickly and easily.

Step 1:

Using your imagination, close your eyes and picture an enormous red stop sign in your mind. Make it as large as the Empire State Building filling your entire mind's eye. Using this stop sign symbolizes you taking action and "stopping" a harmful or negative thought from continuing on its destructive path.

Step 2:

With your eyes closed, consciously "set your intention," or in other words, state the fact that you want to release your negative thought. Simply say to yourself, either aloud or in your mind, whichever is most comfortable for you, "I wish to release this thought."

Step 3:

With your eyes closed, declare that your negative thought no longer serves you. Thank it for any service it did provide for you in the past. Then, let your thought know you no longer need its service. For example, you could say something like, "Thank You for all you have done to help me. However, I no longer need your service. I release you now."

Step 4:

With your eyes closed, create a system for banishing this thought from your mind. If you are a visual person—which means you learn and understand the world around you most easily by seeing pictures or images in your mind—you can "see" this thought surrounded by an army of white knights who run it out of the kingdom of your mind. I encourage you to have fun with this part. Using your amazing imagination, create whatever image works best for you. You have creative freedom to construct it in any way you wish.

Now, if you are more of an auditory person—which means you learn and understand the world around you most easily by hearing it in your mind—then you may use your imagination in order to "hear" your negative thought being banished from your mind. For instance, you could hear trumpets sounding, announcing the banished thought. You could then hear the sound of the horses' feet as the knights charge it out of your mind.

Perhaps you are more of a kinesthetic person—which means you learn and understand the world around you most easily by touching or having a hands-on approach—then you can use your imagination to "feel" with your hands and remove the thought. For example, while you close your eyes, imagine your hands wrapping around the unwanted thought and throwing it away. Then just wipe your hands clean of it.

In the future, should the thought you are working to remove pop up again, simply repeat the above steps. Some thoughts may leave after just one or two times of working through the exercise; other thoughts may take hundreds of tries. Ultimately, you will know when the thought is truly released. You will experience, what I like to call, a shift. You will **simply feel different**. You will feel lighter and witness the rewards of your work in your everyday life. As an example of this, imagine how James' everyday life will change once he completely rids himself of the thought: *Every time I start to have a little enjoyment, it is ruined!* Can you imagine how this will affect everything, from the very little aspects of his life all the way to the big events?

As you put this tool of removing unwanted thoughts into your toolbox, make room for the next tool. You will now learn how to re-script it. By using your imagination, it is time to fill in the space where the unwanted thought once dwelled. This exercise is used so that one harmful thought is not replaced with another. In order to have success with this exercise, the re-scripted thought should directly address the previously held negative or harmful perspective. For example, James' belief *of not being allowed to have any enjoyment in his life* must be replaced with a more positive and uplifting perspective. In this particular instance, I would suggest that James create something along the lines of: *I deserve and allow myself to enjoy my life.* This sentiment will replace his old perception with a fresh one, creating new and positive outcomes. The key to re-scripting is consciously re-writing a negative or harmful thought into a positive, healed, and happy thought.

When using this technique with my clients, they are often initially shy or hesitant to come up with their own re-scripted thoughts. They worry that what they re-script will not be good enough and ask for help. If you are also feeling this way, I encourage you to dive deeply within yourself, because this is where all your answers lie. Everything you need to know and learn is within you. Your inner self is the place where all of the wisdom and strength you will ever need is located.

In order to provide you with a bit of a head start, just as I do with my clients, I have included some generalized re-scripting thoughts below. When beginning the exercise, you may use these as starting points or customize them to fit your exact need. You may not even need them at all. I encourage you to use them if they help and chuck them if they do not. Please remember, having fun with this exercise makes re-scripting a more palatable, enjoyable, and positive experience.

I am lovable.

I am worthy simply because I was created so.

I am loved completely.

I am safe.

Everything is possible.

I can trust myself.

I am valuable.

I count.

I know the right choice for me.

I matter.

I can create a great life for myself.

I am a good person.

I am easy to love.

My dreams are meant to be.

I am surrounded by love and care.

I am capable.

I am whole, complete, and perfect—just as I was created.

I am free.

I allow all goodness to flow into my life.

I am open and receptive to abundance.

I am loved, supported, and guided in every moment.

I am protected.

I am provided for.

I am powerful.

I am good.

I have value.

I have purpose.

I am opening my heart now.

I am expanding in my awareness in every moment.

All is in Divine Order.

I can see Love in all ways.

All is well.

A great phrase to complete any re-scripting thought is to add at the end of it...And So It Is!

The correct re-scripting thoughts are ones that make you feel good when you think of them. If a thought feels good, keep it and apply it. However, if any of your thoughts do not feel encouraging or maybe just mildly so, do not be afraid to chuck them out the window and try again. Keep trying and creating until you feel confident. Trust yourself. You will know the right re-scripting thoughts to use.

Remember, this is your own self-portrait; it can be as magnificently exquisite as you are—it is up to you. Thank God! Thank God, re-scripting your thoughts for your self-portrait is not up to anyone else. There is no other individual in the world who can paint your life portrait as well as you. Only you can create your portrait as the amazing masterpiece you truly are!

You have just accomplished a great deal, learning a substantial number of essential tools. Now, it is time to consciously place these tools in your own personal toolbox. Imagine yourself placing each of these tools, one-by-one, into your personal toolbox. Remember, they are always with you when you need them. They are at your disposal at any time.

Once you have placed your tools into your personal toolbox, I would like you to sit back, relax, and breathe. Using your creative imagination, I would like you to be aware of your breathing. Notice your breath. Notice how your body feels as you breathe. Breathe in all you have learned and processed so far. Allow all of your new tools and knowledge the freedom to integrate into all levels of your consciousness. Slowly breathe in through your nose and out through your mouth. Take three deep cleansing breaths. In through your nose and out through your mouth. As you exhale, allow yourself to make a releasing sound like, A*hhhhhhhh...*

Breathe in through your nose.

Relax.

Breathe out through your mouth.

Relax.

Feel your mind and body settle into a state of acceptance. In your process of healing, know that all you are learning is integrating inside of you now. You are capable of repainting your life portrait. You have what you need within you to accomplish these healing steps.

You are worth it!

Take a deep cleansing breath in…and release.

Yes, that's it.

Relax, breathe, and feel how good that feels!

You may be wondering how we ended up all the way over here, identifying, removing, and re-scripting your thoughts when we were initially discussing how ridiculous it is expecting someone to fix us.

Well, the tools you are learning are a critical part of your road to self-exploration, self-awareness, and self-healing. These tools and exercises, along with all the other tools you will be learning, are what will "fix" you and **not** someone else. These are the things that will set you free to create and enjoy the best life for yourself.

That being said, it is common for most of us to still hold onto the idea that it would be easier for someone outside of ourselves to "fix" us.

So, let us look at this and truly understand that there is not a person outside of ourselves who is capable of "fixing" us.

Imagine you are on your way to work one day and you bump into an incredibly beautiful woman. You share an immediate connection and chemistry. You ask for her number and begin pursuing her. After several dates, she falls madly head-over-heels in love with you. A short time after this occurs she is able to magically figure out all of your issues. From this point on, due to her amazing and special love just for you, she waves her magic love wand and—*POOF!*—you are now whole and complete with not a single issue or unhealed place left within you.

Can you see, hear, and feel how unrealistic and fruitless this expectation actually is?

Now, we will add to this and dive a little deeper into what actually is happening in all relationships. Imagine for a moment that in all of your relationships the other person is merely a full-length mirror.

Throughout the relationship, in all of its interactions, what you are experiencing is a reflection back to you of exactly what is actually going on within you.

This reflection consists of all parts of you; those that are magnificent and awesome and those that are still wounded and need healing. The picture on the outside of you, your external life, is therefore a direct reflection of what is going on inside of you.

When we look at relationships from this perspective, we are able to further explore, understand, and heal those areas we were unaware of or avoiding.

As you come to further understand what relationships are really about, it can sure seem as if we are taking all the "fun" out of getting to blame the other person! Have you ever experienced how great it can feel to point the finger at someone else and say, "It's your fault!...You're to blame!?"

Why, it is a piece of cake!

By doing so, you get to project your own issues onto

another person and not look at yourself or your actions. On the other hand, the healing process requires you to take responsibility for your thoughts, beliefs, actions, words, and life in everything you do.

Not so much fun, right?

Or is it?

Actually, healing can be loads of fun—as long as you can find the fun and humor in each step of the process. Ultimately, the best part is that self-reflection will lead you to live a far more rewarding, enriching, and enjoyable life.

The concept of having fun with such "serious" matters as the healing process might sound a bit counterintuitive. However, having fun with it all is going to make healing that much faster and easier.

I absolutely believe that when we can lighten up and laugh at it all (including ourselves), healing happens more quickly with much more ease and grace.

I have witnessed such success with my clients. Those who can step back, chuckle, shake their heads, and laugh at their issues and themselves move through the process much faster—versus the ones who take everything seriously, creating a heavy and burdensome process.

So, before we move on to the next step and tools, please take some time here to find the humor, fun, and joy in your process.

If you feel yourself becoming bogged down or overwhelmed by it all, just simply stop. Take a well-deserved break.

Find your funny bone and put it to use.

Get silly, shake your head, and laugh it all off.

Remember, you already have everything within you to successfully go through this process—all that is left is simply to laugh!

4

MEETING AND HEALING YOUR INNER CHILD

"One of the virtues of being very young is that you don't let the facts get in the way of your imagination."

Sam Levenson, an American humorist, writer, television host and journalist (1911– 1980)

As you keep your process on the lighter side, you are now ready for the next step in your healing. I will start by stating that most of the time—especially in our relationships—it is not our adult self, but rather our inner child, who is actually running the show.

We all have an inner child. This child is compiled of all of your previous ages and experiences. The inner child can be happy, content, joyful, blissful, excited, creative, imaginative, inspired, loving, tender, kind, generous, brilliant, inquisitive, and an all-around amazing child. At the same time, your inner child can feel scared, sad, lonely, depressed, rejected, abandoned, unloved, unnoticed, insignificant, hurt, abused, small, fearful, and very unsafe.

The inner child is real.

An inner child exists within each of us.

Your inner child is as healthy or unhealthy, or in other words, as functioning or dysfunctional, as was your childhood experience. For instance, if your mother and father were able to provide you with all the love, support, guidance, and inspiration *you individually* needed, your inner child should be functioning quite well. However, if your parent or parents were not capable of providing these things for you, your inner child will experience "wounded parts." You see, in childhood there are normal developmental stages or milestones a child must go through to mature into a healthy adult. If our parent or parents were not aware or capable of helping us go through these stages of normal growth and development, then our inner child becomes emotionally stuck. The place where the child becomes stuck is what I refer to as "wounded parts." In addition, the "wounded parts" cover any and all areas in which a child experienced harm, abuse, or trauma. This harm, abuse, or trauma can be verbal, physical, psychological, or sexual. The good news is, just as wounds on our skin heal, so can our emotional and psychological wounds.

In review, everyone has an inner child and the degree to which an inner child is healthy or unhealthy directly relates to the child's experiences.

To take this to the next step, for every person who did not have their needs met as a child, there is a wounded inner child within them desperately trying to fulfill those needs through their adult relationships. For instance, a man's inner little boy may attract women who are emotionally unavailable. He does this because his mother was emotionally unavailable to him while he was growing up. Attracting this type of relationship gives his inner child the opportunity to continue pursuing emotional connections with an unresponsive woman. In reality, his inner child is searching for the healing that would come from his mommy emotionally showing up for him. Unfortunately, his inner child will continue to be re-traumatized by these types of relationships. This is because he once again will feel defeated in the pursuit of "fixing" what was wrong in his relationship with his mommy.

An example for a woman might be if a little girl felt or actually was abandoned by her father. In adulthood, she then attracts the type of men who will ultimately abandon her. Here again, we can see an example of the inner child mistakenly believing she can "fix" what was wrong with her relationship with her daddy. She believes that if she can successfully get one of these men to stay, she will be okay.

Please understand that most people are unaware that these dynamics play out in their adult relationships. There are very few of us who run around and consciously say to ourselves, *I'm really excited to meet another woman who is emotionally unavailable* or *I can't wait to meet a man who will leave me again, let me get right on that.* No, most of us go through life not knowing this wounded inner child exists, let alone that he/she is controlling the show. Instead, when experiencing cyclical relationship issues, we are more likely to scratch our heads and think, *Why can't I meet the right one?* or *Oh God, why does this always happen?* The irony of this scenario is that these dynamics will continue to play out repeatedly in relationships until the issue is finally recognized. The great news is that once this understanding is achieved, healing the inner child is very possible.

This healing is solely up to you. There is not a person or relationship outside yourself, which can do the healing work for you. This personal responsibility is why the relationship you form with your inner child is **paramount** in the healing process. The inner child affects all areas of your life. When the inner child is in charge, or being the ringleader so to speak, generally our lives are not functioning well because we are operating from wounded parts of the child. Conversely, when our healthy grown-up self or adult mind is in charge, our lives tend to progress very nicely. When working with the inner child, the major goal is to provide healing for those areas in which the inner child is stuck and wounded. Doing so will allow the inner child to grow, mature, and heal. Thus providing You—the adult—the freedom to live a more fulfilling, happy, and healthy life.

By no means, does the healing work with your inner child eliminate the existence of the inner child; it is quite the contrary. The more you heal, the freer you will feel to express all of the wonder and joy of your inner child. You will find that you are better able to experience all sorts of playing, creating, laughing, and fun!

Working with your inner child begins with the simple step of getting to know your inner child. This starts as it would in any type of new relationship. To begin, the following exercise will allow you the chance to be introduced to your inner child. As the exercise continues, we will take each step one-by-one. Along the way, you will be actively participating, which means you will place this book down and actually do the exercise, so you may connect with your inner child. In order for you to receive the most benefit out of this tool, please employ this exercise during a time and in a space where you can be quiet, alone, and comfortable. I will describe in advance everything you will need to know to participate in the exercise. From there, you simply follow the steps and when prompted, close your eyes, and begin the process. When you have completed the exercise, simply resume reading for the next step.

First, we will simply say, *Hello*.

Most of the time, your inner child will present himself to you at the age where he feels most comfortable. Whatever the age or manner in which your inner child reveals himself is great. In order to accomplish this initial meeting, we are going to set up a safe place within your mind to have this introduction. We will do this simply by using your imagination. You can do this in any way you feel comfortable. You can see, hear, or feel this space. There is no one correct method. Some people experience seeing and hearing the inner child. Others cannot see or hear but rather feel the inner child. Again, whichever way you feel comfortable doing this exercise is the appropriate healing method for you.

Now, let's begin:

You will be using your most vivid imagination in order to create what I like to call your *white room*. As alluded to in the name, the room you create in your mind is entirely white. The walls are white. The floors are white. The ceiling is white. This white room is absolutely perfect for you. Its size and shape are whatever will be most comfortable for you. It is big enough for you to feel open and free. It is small enough for you to feel safe, cozy, and protected. The room is uncluttered by any furniture or possessions. There are many large windows allowing a steady stream of golden-white light to illuminate the room. The abundance of this light fills your white room with complete warmth, guidance, and Love. This room is a very special and unique place. It is always completely safe and a place where you are constantly protected, provided for, cared for, nurtured, and unconditionally loved in every moment. If you can imagine a time when you felt this way, use that specific experience and expand on it. If you cannot imagine such a time or have not had such an experience, then you can use the image of what I refer to as the: *Womb of God…Womb of the Creator…Womb of the Universe…*or *Womb of the Divine.*

In this image, you can use your imagination and create all the benefits of a womb: provision, nurturing, safety, growth, and protection. However, this environment is even greater than a real womb. Here, the environment is entirely filled with the perfect amount of light and all the safety, comfort, care, nurturing, and Love *you individually* will ever need or desire. If you do not connect with this image and it does not help you envision your white room, then simply sit with your thoughts for a while in order to discover what image or sense of being works for you here. This is your white room and it is for You in whichever way works best.

Once you have a clear picture, sense, or feel of your white room, it is time for you to meet your inner child. After you continue reading the following steps, you will be prompted when to begin the exercise.

In your mind, you will bring to your awareness your personal white room. Then, simply enter into the room. If you become stuck, just remember this is all in your imagination and you have control. Now, as you enter—feel, see, hear, or sense yourself in the room. Simply experience the occurrence of yourself in this wonderful place. Embrace how this white room feels for you. Notice what thoughts you may be having. As well, pay attention to how your body and emotions feel. Now, it is time to intend to meet your inner child. This step means: simply be open and willing to meet with your inner child. Consciously choose to feel yourself opening up to this experience. Allow yourself to experience this exercise with practical ease. From this point, simply and warmly say aloud, *Hello.* Then, just be still and present in the moment. Your inner child may show up right away or it may take a few moments. Either way is okay. Stay present in the moment and stay present with the exercise, so your inner child may have the opportunity to present himself. Once you meet your inner child, let him know you are here for him now. Let him know you are learning how to be present for him in all ways. Let him know this is only the beginning and you are excited to build a great relationship with him. Once you have done this, let your inner child know there is an "auto-play" button that you are pushing, so that you and he are always here in this amazingly safe and Love-filled space together. Tell him that from this moment on, he is never alone. You are always with him even when you are consciously living in your adult life. Display for him you pushing the "auto-play" button and help him understand this means you are always with him. Once you feel he understands this concept, slowly open your eyes then bring your awareness back to the moment and continue reading.

Rereading the above steps several times will help prepare you for this exercise. Once you feel ready, place this book down and begin your process with this exercise.

How did you do?

Did your inner child arrive?

If not, do not worry. I would like for you now to get up, stretch, move around, shake your limbs, take some deep breaths in through your nose, and out through your mouth. Relax. Breathe. Actively release any mental or emotional blocks you may be having to this experience. Directly address any thought or belief that may be holding you back from this wonderful experience. Such thoughts may sound something like:

This is stupid.

This will never work.

This is psycho-mumbo-jumbo.

This is ridiculous.

I can't do this!

Whatever the blocking thought or thoughts may be, simply release the thought and invite yourself to suspend any fear or cynicism, in order to perform this exercise. Think of the experience as a new adventure—not something so serious. Let go and allow the moment in.

Now it is time to retry this step. Place yourself gently back into your white room and start the process again. Remember to breathe and relax all along the way.

Once you have successfully met with your inner child, it is time to get your personal notebook out and answer the following questions. As you consider each question, make sure to stay consciously aware and act as the objective observer of you. Pay particular attention to what and how you are feeling.

How old was my inner child when he appeared to me?

What did my inner child look like?

What clothes was my inner child wearing?

What was the emotional state of my inner child?

Did I recognize my inner child?

How did I feel meeting my inner child?

What emotions came up for me during this process?

Did my inner child seem to be open to meeting me?

What aspect of this first meeting felt most important to me?

Following your initial introduction with your inner child, you are now going to spend a little quality time with him. On the other hand, you may feel as if the first experience was enough for now and you want a break. If you need a break, I encourage you to take one. However, resuming this work with your inner child as quickly as you can is best for optimum results.

For the second step, you will return to your white room. This time, you will place a big comfortable play area in the middle of your white room. Your play area can be any size, shape, color, or type.

I. Once you have chosen the perfect play area for you, simply place it in the middle of the floor in your white room. Consciously remember how this room feels. Feel yourself experience the warmth, safety, provision, and Love filling this room. Allow all of the Love, care, and support to envelop you. Breathe all of it in. Breathe in through your nose and out through your mouth. When you have found yourself completely and comfortably immersed in this space, it is then time to ask your inner child to come and visit with you in the play area. He may arrive immediately, or may be a bit shy and take a while.

II. In either case, when your inner child arrives, simply ask him what he would like to have in this play area. It can be absolutely anything. I mean anything! You can offer any type of food, drink, stuffed animals, toy figures, model airplanes, cars, trucks, games, a horse, candy, a roller coaster, books, or simply nothing at all. Again, whatever your inner child wants is what you immediately provide. Always make sure, though, your offering is in his best interest and will not cause him any harm. For instance, if your inner child asks for firecrackers, you can gently and lovingly explain how real firecrackers can burn him and that this would not be safe for him. Then explain that here in this special place he can have very unique firecrackers which will not burn him. If he does not like that idea, help him think of something else he would like instead of the real firecrackers. This nurturing act of compromise helps establish you as the parent, as well as helping him feel safe within the boundaries you set for him.

III. Once your inner child communicates with you what he would like to have in the play area, allow your amazing imagination to provide this for him. You do not have to force anything here. Have fun with this! Once you have everything he wants on the play area—watch and witness him fully enjoying all he requested. Spend this quality time with him, consciously connecting with him. Your time together can be filled with playing, eating, laughing, silence, tears, wrestling, hugging, reading, running around, or any combination of these experiences. The main goal of this step is to *allow* anything your inner child needs to actually occur. There are no rules, laws, or restrictions here. In this space, all things are possible. You and your inner child can float, fly, paint, play, and defy all the rules of this world. Set you and your inner child free to be happy and joyful. Allow your inner child to share with you whatever he would like to experience. Then, let your imagination break free and wildly create it to be!

I do not want to project anything into or onto your unique experience with your inner child by sharing with you what commonly happens with most inner children. However, I will share with you that as long as your inner child feels happy and content; he is in a good place for you to come back to your conscious awareness in your adult mind.

IV. When you feel as if your inner child is saturated with this experience, meaning he is finished sharing this time with you, show him that you are pushing the "auto-play" button and remind him that you are always here for him and he is never alone. This action is very important to do each time you visit your inner child.

When you complete this part of the exercise, I encourage you once again to check in with yourself and see if you need a break, or if you are ready to keep reading. Whatever you need is perfectly fine to do. Only you can determine what is best for you. A good yardstick of measuring how you are doing in the process is checking if you feel you are truly getting a sense and understanding of your inner child. Up to this point, the inner child work you have completed is the foundation for a positive and healthy relationship for you both. As this relationship grows, you will experience a profound emotional shift. The shift will occur within your personal awareness, insights, and understanding of yourself and those around you.

You are now prepared to complete this next step in your process with your inner child. Simply review the above guidance.

Place this book down…close your eyes…and begin.

I hope your experience was a good one and that you are really feeling closer to your inner child.

Since this work is so very vital, before continuing with further reading and going on to the next steps of our process, I **highly recommend** you stop reading and repeat the entire inner child step in your play area, once a day, for a minimum of one full week.

Each day of the following week, allow yourself at least five full minutes to participate and fully engage with your inner child. With each experience, the goal is to become closer and closer to your inner child.

Developing a more intimate bond with your inner child is necessary in order to move forward in the healing process. If at the end of the week you feel you are not quite ready to move forward with learning a new exercise, please take all the time you need before moving on. When I work directly with a client, building the inner child relationship can sometimes take up to a few months at a time. So, please only move forward when you are ready. At the same time, consistency and continuity in this work are just as important.

Welcome back!

How was your experience last week?

Were you able to devote five full minutes a day to your inner child? If so, you and your inner child are most likely connecting. This connection helps your inner child to learn to trust you. This trust is the springboard from which substantial healing will take off. If you are unable to do this yet, it is all right. This is your process and it happens in your time and at your pace. Relax, take it slowly, and just continue to repeat the steps until you feel the connection with your inner child. If you continue to do the exercises, you will get there—do not despair or give up. It will happen for you!

As you are emotionally connecting with your inner child, you are ready for the third step. This exercise is a little more complex, because it has a couple different layers to explore:

I. To start, I would like you to turn on your creative imagination and paint the most vivid and picturesque private beach scene possible. Create all of the elements—the water, the air, the sun, the sand, the waves, and the temperature perfectly to your liking. Make sure all the child-ready elements are present, as well. For instance, fill your beach scene with an abundance of bright, colorful sand and water toys. You might want to include in this scene: floats, rafts, surfboards, boogie boards, boats, kites, umbrellas, masks, snorkels, balls, volleyball nets, bathing suits, balloons, soft beach towels, and lots of tasty food, ice cold drinks, and treats.

II. After you set the scene, simply invite your inner child to join you. Allow your inner child to arrive in any manner he would like. After arriving, ask your inner child to show you what he would like to play with first. Follow your inner child's lead.

Play.

Play.

Play.

Let go and freely play. Run around and laugh together. Feel the joy. It is all there for you now. Go ahead. Play!

III. As you continue to participate in this exercise, it is time to initiate direct dialogue with your inner child. Begin by asking some general questions, such as:

Are you having fun?

What would you like to do next?

Do you like when we play together?

After asking your inner child each question—listen. He will start to share with you. Once your inner child does open up, continue with the following question: "Is there anything you need to tell me or show me that is bothering you?" Whatever "it" is, inform your inner child you will do whatever it takes to make it all better.

Then, do it!

Remember, just like your white room, all things are possible here. There are no rules, laws, or restrictions in this space. Act as if you are the all-powerful parent, able to fix anything and everything for your child. Then, simply fix it! I want you to show up BIG here for your inner child. Show up and save the day! Be the superhero for him. By doing so, you will further cement the bond and trust, which will help further you along to the next step. Do not worry if this exercise feels strange or uncomfortable. That is normal. Simply keep going—it is all okay! As a gentle reminder, please always show your inner child that you are pushing the "auto-play" button. This is very important to do each time you work with your inner child.

Ready?

Set?

Place this book down…

Create!

How did it go? If you are feeling great, you are ready for the next step. If it did not go as planned, then that is okay, too. Everything is as it should be. You are experiencing your healing work in exactly the way that is perfect for you. Do not push or force this process—remember to breathe and allow the moment to happen. Just start from the beginning and try again.

Remember, everything is possible here. You have the ability within you to manifest every solution your inner child seeks. Perhaps your inner child is feeling scared about a past memory. Whatever the situation, you can go in and fix it. For example, if your inner child is feeling unsafe, provide the exact circumstances for him to feel safe. Perhaps you do so by creating a personal white room just for your inner child. Then accompany him there. You may hold, rock, cradle, sing to, assure, and comfort him. What would have made you feel safe when you were a child? Find that safety and simply provide it. Maybe your inner child is feeling scared of someone, such as a parent, bully, relative, coach, or teacher. In this case, your inner child could grow to the size of an enormous giant. Then, you can have the person he is afraid of reduced in size to a microscopic particle and dissipate into thin air. If your inner child is feeling lonely, you could throw a huge "We Love You" party in his honor. Fill the party with all the people who love your inner child. Then, bring in the golden-white light streaming through the windows. See and feel the light fill your party and envelop your inner child.

By trusting in yourself, it will be revealed to you exactly what you need to do for your inner child. Try again and you will succeed.

Up to this point, you have been introduced to and have met your inner child. As well, you have established a rapport and are building a sound relationship with your inner child. Now, we are going to establish more concretely your role in the ongoing relationship with your inner child. Your role is to show up and act as the "perfect" parent.

Do perfect parents exist in real life?

No!

Can parents do a pretty amazing job?

Yes!

Your job here is to be the perfect parent to your inner child. You are capable of doing this because you are using your imagination in a space free of any and all rules, laws, or restrictions. All children, including your inner child, need unconditional love, acceptance, nurturing, to feel seen, to feel they matter, to feel heard, to have boundaries, to have encouragement, to feel supported, and have all the guidance they need. All children also need food, clothing, exercise, shelter, an education, and creative outlets. In addition, all children need discipline. The way in which the word *discipline* is used varies among people. The way I use the word discipline means *to teach*. This form of discipline has nothing to do with hitting, forcing, intimidating, or hurting a child into submission. All children need to be taught what is healthy and supports them, as well as those things that can cause them harm. This teaching should occur from the time of infancy through early adulthood.

How many parents do you know, maybe including yourself, who have perfectly taught their children everything? How many parents have attended parenting classes to learn all the developmental stages of childhood? How many parents swear they will do it differently but end up raising their children in the same manner, as did their own parents? Even the most educated parents with the best intentions make mistakes. Little mistakes or big ones, we all do it. The best way out of this trap is to understand and know yourself so well that you do not repeat the mistakes of your parents or your own past. Fortunately, this understanding is what you are currently in the midst of achieving. This experiencing and exploring into yourself not only brings with it healing for yourself, it positively affects those around you and the generations to come.

Can you recall all the ways in which your parents served you well? Can you bring to your conscious awareness all the ways and means by which your parents positively assisted you along your journey of growing up? This is a good time to get your notebook out and write down all the ways, memories, and times you can remember your parents providing love, guidance, and lessons that helped you most. In addition, take this time to record all those moments and ways in which they did not. By writing out your memories, both positive and negative, you will be provided with the opportunity to gain even more personal insight. As well, you will be learning more ways you can help to heal your inner child. By no means is this an exercise meant to point the finger at or blame your parents. This is simply to assist you in understanding what worked for you as a child and what did not.

Now, think about what you would consider your picture-perfect parents to be. What does this picture look like for you? Spend some time on the details. Ask yourself, "How would my perfect mother and father look? How would they act? How would they treat me, view me, and parent me?"

Imagine in front of you, a scale from one to one hundred. Now, place your "perfect parents" on the one-hundred mark and your actual parents on the mark where you would rank them. This exercise is not meant to blame, shame, or chastise your actual parents in any way. You are simply being honest with yourself and deciding where you would rank the parenting you received. Now look at the difference between the two rankings. The amount of distance between these two sets of parents is the exact amount of parenting your inner child needs to have you provide for him. For example, if you rank your parents at the thirty percent mark that would mean that there is seventy percent of parenting your inner child needed that he did not receive. Again, it is very important that we use this tool as a simple guide and not a "blame game." All of our parents truly did the best they could with what they had at the time. Bless them and thank them for what they were able to give you and quickly move your attention to the re-parenting of your inner child. As you continue parenting your inner child, you can use this scale as a personal reference point to measure the progress and healing you make. While going along, it can be very helpful to draw this scale in your personal notebook and keep it as a reminder within your notes.

You are now ready for the fourth step in working with your inner child. As you continue working with him, now is the time to embody the role of the perfect parent. At this point in the process, I recommend you spend at least five full minutes each day with your inner child. During this five-minute exercise, simply inquire how your inner child is doing. Ask your inner child how he is and discover if there is anything your inner child needs from you. Within this interaction is where you become the perfect parent. As long as your inner child's needs are healthy and positively support him in an affirming way, show up big, and provide them. If what your inner child wants is harmful to him or someone else, now is your chance to teach him and employ boundaries. Provide whatever is necessary to help him understand the boundaries you are putting into place for him.

Here is an example:

> You check in with your inner child and he is angry with another child in school. This child is a bully and torments your inner child. Your inner child wants to retaliate by physically harming this bully. As the perfect parent, you validate your inner child's feelings, saying something like: *I understand you are feeling angry at so-and-so for bullying you. I would feel the same way. However, in our family we do not hit others. When we are angry, we talk about it, understand it, forgive it, and then move on. So, let's talk about it. Tell me everything you are feeling and we will find a solution together.*

From this point on, you listen to your inner child and teach him what he needs to learn and understand. You affirm, guide, love, and assure him. You nurture him and provide him with all he needs. Always remember—with this work, you can do anything!

This inner work with your own inner child is such a significant part of your healing process. Checking in with him daily and "parenting" him in the specific way he needs is absolutely vital. As you continue to work with him, you will be able to witness how he will become more and more healed. You will feel the shift occur as he is provided the opportunity to grow, mature, and move past the wounds into a healed place.

The reason you are now stepping into this "parenting" role is not only to help your inner child, but also to help yourself in your adult life.

If you ever hear yourself saying something like, *I need you to act this way______,* know it is the voice of your wounded inner child. If you catch yourself saying, *If you loved me, you would_____,* you are witnessing the voice of your inner child.

An adult—a healthy, well-adjusted, functioning adult—would never utter such words, sentiments, or expectations. Speaking in this manner would not occur to such an adult, because emotionally healthy adults understand and live from an awareness that everything comes from within. In other words, they are operating from an internal locus of control, rather than an external locus of control. These adults understand there is nothing outside of themselves that they need. They may desire certain things or circumstances, but they do not need them. They have a deep relationship with themselves and take accountability for their thoughts, feelings, and actions. Healthy adults do not look for others to save, rescue, fix, or love them into happiness. They understand that achieving inner peace and experiencing happiness is an "inside job."

Now, for the rest of us—those of us who have had less than perfect childhoods, who have no idea how to have or function in an intimate, healthy relationship, and who desperately want to learn—let us remember how far we have come:

> **First**, you now know the relationship you form with yourself is the most important one you will ever have. Setting the tone for everything else in your life, you know this relationship must be established, maintained, and nurtured.

> **Second**, you have learned to become consciously aware and act as the objective observer of you. As well, you are employing these tools on a daily basis.

> **Third**, you are taking what you learn from being consciously aware and acting as the objective observer, and are intentionally removing and re-scripting unwanted, harmful thoughts and beliefs.

> **Fourth**, you have established a relationship with your inner child. You are sustaining and nurturing this connection on a daily basis.

Fantastic!

Look how far you have come already!

Now, all you have to do is continue to use these tools on a daily basis. Simply carry them around with you in your toolbox and put them into practice, as you need them.

You have the ability to heal, grow, expand, and create peace in your own life—both internally and externally. When you have mastered these tools, you will feel an internal shift and witness an external shift in your life. This shift comes in the form of you feeling a newfound lightness, with more ability to experience happiness, joy, and peace in your daily life.

5

NURTURING YOUR INTIMATE RELATIONSHIP

"If you judge people, you have no time to love them."

Mother Teresa (1910 - 1997)

We now come to the part of your healing process in which we will address your intimate relationship. As you read this section, please know that most of this information can also be applied to all of the relationships you have in your life.

First, let us start with the question, *What is a relationship really all about?* There are many theories and belief systems built around this exact question. Many believe that an intimate relationship is a place in which they get all their needs met. Others believe an intimate relationship is the place where they will find their "other half." While others believe, it is the most important relationship they will ever have in their life. In my personal and professional experience, I have found there are two main components defining our intimate relationships. The first component provides us with an environment in which we are able to act as "mirrors" for one another. The second component provides us with the opportunity to experience lots and lots of joy, co-creation, and love!

The first element, acting as "mirrors" for one another, is often misunderstood and misused because most people are unaware of this facet of the relationship.

Imagine for a moment that your significant other is standing right there in front of you. Now, imagine that instead of seeing your partner, you see a large full-length mirror instead. You can no longer "see" her, but instead you see a reflection of yourself.

Now, imagine that she has shown up in your life to act as a teacher and guide for you. Her job is to hold up this mirror for you, so that you may recognize for yourself all of the magnificence and glory that is *you*. As well, the mirror is there so you may be able to understand the wounded areas within you that simply need healing. Now, I would like you to imagine that most of the time she is not acting as a mirror on a conscious level and is generally unaware of this dynamic herself.

To more fully understand the concept of "mirrors," I want you to imagine the exact scenario for your partner. Imagine that you are a full-length mirror for her, reflecting back all she needs to see and discover about herself. Imagine you have showed up in her life to be a teacher and guide for her and for the most part, you are not doing this on a conscious level either.

We are going to do a little exercise with this new

information. First, jot down all the ways in which you have seen your magnificence reflected back to you by your partner. Be sure to be specific with the circumstances and times when this has occurred. For example, those times when you have seen, heard, or felt from your partner how amazing and wonderful you are. Once you have completed this part of the exercise, for the second step, write about the times in which you feel your wounded places have been reflected back to you. This one is a little more complicated because it requires you to really look at yourself with authentic and honest vision—to see those "ugly" parts of your portrait, which are not always easy to view.

Once you have completed both parts of this exercise, it is now time to switch it around. This time you will write down how you feel you have reflected back to your partner all of her magnificence, as well as her wounds. Take as long as you need to complete this exercise, so you may discover important information about your intimate relationship and yourself.

Once you complete the steps in this exercise, continue reading...

Were you able to recall and figure out the "mirrors" in your intimate relationship?

Just as with all the tools you have learned about thus far, the more you practice this tool, the easier it will become. When you employ your new "mirror approach" with your intimate relationship and all your relationships for that matter, a world of information about yourself becomes readily available to you—if you are willing to look at it. This occurs because the mirror tool transforms the more common dynamic of the "blame game"—where we blame and project out onto our partners those places in us that need healing—to a healthier and healing path of self-discovery. The next time you are irritated or upset with your partner, imagine that you remember she is simply showing up for you as a teacher and guide in the form of a full-length mirror. From this place, can you imagine what you will be privy to? It is a world of incredibly valuable information.

Now, let us move on to the second component of an intimate relationship. This element is the place where you and your partner have the opportunity to experience great joy, co-creation, and love!

To begin, you and your partner will *hold the space* for the greatest good for one another. This means that neither of you will try to "get" anything from the other. Rather, you will both provide love from a place of giving and service. Secondly, you will bear witness to and celebrate each other's magnificence. You will be able to walk side-by-side—honoring, supporting, and sharing your growth, experiences, and creations with one another, all in selfless love.

Doesn't that sound great?

It *is* great! Those who master these tools experience the most remarkable relationships.

Let us look at a simple example displaying the possibilities within this second element of the intimate relationship. In order to make the information very clear, I will present two hypothetical scenes. As you read each of them, remember to stay consciously aware and act as the objective observer of you.

Let us start with the first scene:

George comes home from work and is feeling quite beaten up by the day. His wife, Trudy, is just getting in the door, as well. Her day was not as bad as George's day, but she is tired and worn out just the same. They greet one another with a quick peck and each goes off in different directions to change their clothes, check emails, and return phone calls. Meanwhile, they decide to order-in for dinner. When the food arrives, George and Trudy collapse on the couch with plates in hand and watch television. Before long, they get ready for bed. As they say goodnight to one another, George—suddenly feeling in the mood—makes his usual move on Trudy. He grabs her breast and pulls her close. This does nothing at all for Trudy, except anger her. She immediately pulls away and snaps at George. Feeling rejected and even more beaten up, he rolls over and falls asleep only to start the same day all over again tomorrow. Trudy, who is now feeling very unloved and like a "piece of meat," rolls over and falls asleep as well.

Before reading the second example, let us pretend this will be a scene in a movie. You are now the writer and director. Imagine for a moment what direction you would give to George and Trudy. For this exercise, tap into your most creative imagination and all of the tools you have learned so far. What would your scene look like?

Now, let us re-write this scene together.

First, let us make sure George and Trudy are each doing their own personal inner work. Then, let us have George and Trudy come home in the same emotional states:

George is feeling beaten up and Trudy is feeling tired and worn out. However, this time when they greet one another, they take a moment; look deeply into one another's eyes and say, *Hello*—they are *witnessing* each other. Then, when the food is delivered, they choose to sit down together. They proceed to have a real dialogue about their experiences during the day. Each shares what they enjoyed, what they were grateful for, and the areas of the day where they struggled. As each person shares his or her experiences and feelings, the other really listens attentively with great care—they are *holding the space* for one another. As each finishes sharing, the other asks, *How can I support you in this?*—they are *giving and being in service with one other,* from a place of love and support.

How do you feel reading this scene?

Do you like it? Do you feel it is possible?

Can you imagine your partner and you behaving this way with one another?

Your answers to these questions are very important. The ability to imagine and know this type of relationship is possible is the key for being able to make it happen. Take a few moments here to envision treating your partner and yourself with this love, honor, support, and gentle care. How do you feel your internal and external life would be different from what it is now?

Now, take a few more moments to think about some goals you may have for yourself in your intimate relationship. These goals can include anything you feel would improve the quality of your intimate relationship. For example, you may come up with the idea that you would like to work on *witnessing* your partner. From here, you can set a goal that each time you see her you will *witness* her. This means that you will take her in—all of her—all of the wonder of her and the wounds within her. With this goal in mind, you choose to "see" her with eyes of compassion and love. You also choose to reflect this back to her through your actions, feelings, or simply with your presence.

During this part of the healing process, I often hear from my clients, "Bree, can't you just give me a simple outline to help me with my relationship?" I believe this question often comes from a pure place of frustration with just not knowing how or what to do in an intimate relationship.

To explore what I mean, let us first review what we have just discussed. I believe there are two main components in an intimate relationship.

The first component, being a "mirror" for one another, takes a real shift in perception and the ability to be truly authentic with yourself. The second component consists of being consciously aware and taking loving care of your partner and yourself. From here, we will discover a useful and applicable "outline" to help assist you with your intimate relationship. As you are well aware, staying consciously aware and acting as the objective observer of you is vital. Also, remember to stay aware of your inner child, his needs, and any negative or harmful thoughts, which need removing and re-scripting.

The relationship "outline" I have developed starts with a very simple premise:

I have found that most men and women would like to feel good with and around their partners.

Wow! Imagine that! We all want to feel good in our relationships! Can it really be that simple? Yes. I believe it's that simple!

The following "outline" is set up with the three simple desires most men and women would like to have met in their intimate relationship.

It is important that we each understand what the other desires. Through this understanding comes the ability to meet these desires from a conscious place of love and support.

A man desires…

I. Good food

II. Good sex with *his* woman

III. To feel that *his* woman thinks he is the greatest man in the world

A woman desires…

I. To feel loved by *her* man

II. To feel beautiful and desired by *her* man

III. To feel safe and provided for by *her* man

I know what you are thinking, *It's that simple? That's it? Are you crazy?!* Seriously, male and female desires really are that simple. When you boil down all the other issues of the relationship, most men and women would like these simple desires met by their partners. Meanwhile, the other parts of the relationship; the deeper more profound parts—such as wanting to share in meaningful existential or spiritual conversations or the superficial parts of the relationship—such as how hot their partner looks in a bathing suit, are simply the added whip cream and cherry on top.

When you have two healthy, functioning adults living their lives from an internal locus of control and wholeness, who are treating one another and themselves with love, honor, and gentle care and then you add to that each one providing the above simple desires—you have the recipe for a successful relationship!

We will first look at the female desires in more detail:

A Woman desires...

I. To Feel Loved by *Her* Man

Love simply *is*. It just *is*. Either you love or you do not love. Either you are coming from a place of love or you are not. Love *is*. You do not have to earn it, perform for it, pay a price for it, or struggle to get it. Love *is*. There are, however, different ways in which people *understand, feel, and express* love.

While love simply *is*, we all understand, feel, and express love in particular ways. One form of expression is not better than another, just different. What makes one person feel loved could do absolutely nothing for another person and vice-versa. To have a healthy relationship with yourself, you must understand how you feel loved. At the same time, to have a healthy intimate relationship, each partner must understand how the other feels and expresses love.

There is a general rule of thumb, which states: *The way people want to receive physically is usually the way they will give physically.* Well, that same rule of thumb can be applied here in how we express our love to one another. Usually, people express their love to others in the exact way they understand and feel loved. In order to discover how you feel loved, as you read the following questions, ask yourself: *Is this the way I feel loved?*

Do you feel loved when…

Someone pays attention to you?

Someone looks in your eyes and says he/she loves you?

Someone is thoughtful and shows kindness to you?

Someone says complimentary and loving things to you?

You are being held?

You spend time with someone?

You have fun and play with someone?

Someone gives you a gift?

Someone supports your passion and heart's desires?

Someone believes in your dreams?

Someone treats you with admiration and respect?

Someone pursues you and wants to spend quality time with you?

Someone writes you love letters?

Once you have answered these questions, I would like you to ask yourself, *How do I express my love to my partner?* More often than not, we do express our love to our partner in the way *we* understand and feel loved.

After you have explored and developed a clear understanding of how you feel loved, it is time to find out and understand how your woman feels loved. While this step might seem difficult, it does not have to be complicated or intense. Simply ask your women, "Honey, how do you feel loved?" If she has a hard time answering the question, you can show her the above list of questions to help her identify exactly how she feels loved. As well, share with her the general rule of thumb previously mentioned.

Now that you each are clear on how you individually feel loved, you can move into the next step. This next step is positive reinforcement. This means that you positively reinforcing the behaviors you would like to have continued. For example, let us say you discover you feel loved when your woman hugs you. From now on, when she hugs you, positively reinforce her behavior by letting her know how good it feels for you. You could do this by saying something like, "Honey, I feel so loved when you hug me." Another example of this could be when she tells you how great she thinks you are. You could positively reinforce this behavior by saying something like, "Honey, I feel so good when you tell me such nice things, thank you so much!" The more you practice reinforcing this behavior, the better she will be at providing it for you. This tool works for you, as well. Once you know and understand the ways in which your woman feels loved, the more you can express love to her in the way she receives it best.

Remember, it is simple.

We all want to be and feel loved and when we receive expressions of love in the way we understand it best, it feels good!

A Woman desires...

II. To Feel Beautiful and Desired by *Her* Man

When a woman feels and receives affirmation from her man that she is beautiful and desired, she is set free to express all of who she is within the relationship. I am not talking about a man *making* a woman feel beautiful or desirable, for that is impossible. A man cannot make a woman feel something she does not already feel within herself. In order to feel beautiful and desired, a woman must first know and feel she is beautiful and desirable. Remember, all relationships are really a mirror reflecting back to us those areas within ourselves that are to be celebrated, enjoyed, recognized, and healed.

What does it mean to you, "Beauty is in the eye of the beholder?" How much do you value inner beauty?

Have you ever been in the presence of a woman who,

by societal standards, would not be considered beautiful? However, once you got to know her, who she was as a person was so beautiful, she was radiant? On the other hand, have your ever witnessed a woman who, by societal standards, was considered to be extremely beautiful, but as soon as she opened her mouth that "beauty" disappeared right before your eyes?

This concept, beauty, how would you define it?

How does a man communicate to his woman that she is beautiful and he desires her? Some men are born with this gift. It comes so naturally for them that they do not even have to try. Appreciation and acknowledgement instinctively pours out of their words and actions towards her. This type of man can just look at his woman from across a crowded room and she feels as if she is the only woman in the room and the only woman in the world for him.

What does this type of man do to create this experience?

I believe it is because he looks **into** his woman instead of **at** her. He beholds all of her incredible beauty. He witnesses her inner and outer beauty and delights in it. She can feel from him that he is her greatest fan and celebrates in every aspect of her. He knows how blessed he is to have her and she can feel this belief emanate from him.

But what about all the other men who were not born with

this natural gift?

Generally, when a man is in love and committed to a woman, he wants to do what he can to make her feel beautiful and desired. However, if a man does not have the skills or has never been taught how to express his feelings and love, he can be left feeling frustrated and as if he has failed his woman.

When this happens, what is a man to do?

Does this sound familiar to your situation?

Do you sometimes feel as though you are communicating your love and desire for her, but she does not understand or know how to receive it?

If so, you are not alone.

Communicating love and desire, in ways our partner can understand, is an ongoing challenge in most relationships.

I believe that most men, when given the chance, want to learn how to provide what their women desire.

This eagerness is a powerful tool, because all it takes is a little bit of willingness to learn how to communicate your love and desire!

To get started, I recommend using the following steps to help you fulfill the first two desires.

1. Identify and understand how you feel loved.
2. Identify and understand how your woman feels loved.
3. Communicate with your woman so together you can come up with practical ways each of you can express your love.
4. Positively reinforce these behaviors.
5. Ask your woman how she feels beautiful and desired by you.
6. Actively listen to her response. If she struggles with this question, ask her specifically, "Honey, when I tell you that you look beautiful, do you feel beautiful and desired by me?" Then listen some more. Help her by expressing to her how willing you are to learn.
7. Then, put into action on a consistent and daily basis what you have just learned about her.
8. Finally, enjoy the fruits of your labor! Watch and see how she will blossom in your midst!

A Woman desires…

III. To Feel Safe and Provided for by *Her* Man

A woman's third simple desire in her intimate relationship, to feel safe and provided for by her man, may sound too old fashioned for today's woman. At first glance, I agree. However, when we dissect this desire it makes a lot of sense.

A woman can feel safe and provided for with a man in different ways:

She can feel safe and provided for physically.

She can feel safe and provided for emotionally.

She can feel safe and provided for financially.

A woman **feels safe and provided for physically** with a man when she knows, no matter what, he will never use his physical force to harm her in any way. She also wants to know and feel he will use his physical force to always protect and help her in any way he can.

For example:

One night while you and your woman are walking down a street, she hears a noise, becomes frightened, and jumps. You look around, observe where the noise came from, reassure her everything is okay, and escort her to safety.

Or perhaps:

Your woman is working on a painting project on your formal living room's fourteen-foot high ceilings. You walk into the living room and notice she can only reach and paint to within two feet of the ceiling. Immediately concerned that she might fall off the ladder and hurt herself, you gladly offer your help and finish the project for her.

Or physical safety may even look this simple:

As you walk through a crowded room together, you gently place your hand on the small of her back and guide her through the crowd.

A woman can **feel safe and provided for emotionally** with her man when she knows no matter what she has to share with him, he will be present with her by listening attentively with interest, respect, and concern.

For example:

During an intimate conversation, she shares with you her innermost fears. Throughout her sharing, you listen without interrupting, validate her feelings when she is done, and do not try to "fix" it for her. If she cries, you hold her as she lets it all out.

The natural and immediate response in most men is to fix a problem when presented with one. However, when a woman is sharing her feelings with you, she just wants to be heard. She does not want to be told how to fix it or that you will fix it for her. This one definitely takes some getting used to for most men. However, when you do it, you will see how much better it will turn out for you both.

Another example:

Your woman, having a very trying day at work with her co-workers, is looking forward to venting with you. She calls and tells you all about the unfair and backstabbing treatment she received all day. You listen, wait until she is finished with her story, and then side with her about how awful her co-workers were to her. You then lighten the mood by finding the humor in it and you both start to laugh about how ridiculous it all is. You remind her of how wonderful you think she is and ask her in a humorous way if she wants you to go beat them up.

When it comes to a woman **feeling safe and provided for financially** with a man, for the most part, we are past the point where a woman is considered a possession owned by her man. However, just as a man still has that primal, biological drive to spread his seed, a woman has the primal desire to feel that you can protect and provide for her and her children.

That being said, in today's society, although the way a

woman feels safe and provided for financially with a man has changed, the desire for this has not.

Most women not only know they are capable of providing for themselves and their children; they are doing so. Unlike previous generations, women today are experiencing prosperous careers, raising children, taking care of the home, and finding some time for their personal lives. While this is an amazing feat, I challenge you to this one question: Are women doing this well? What I mean is, can a woman, or man for that matter, can any one person do all of this at the same time and do it all well?

I do believe women are doing the very best they can to provide for themselves, their partner, and their children. However, when we take a closer look at the full picture, we see the parts and pieces of their career, home, and personal life that are suffering.

How could they not?

How can one person handle all these responsibilities *and* do it all one-hundred percent, one-hundred percent of the time? In most cases, I believe something eventually has to give, to ease the burden. I completely support women's rights and women's liberation. The freedom and benefits women enjoy today because of this movement are profound and were very necessary. Unfortunately, the negative impacts are being ignored. In our society, it is almost taboo to talk about this perspective of the feminist movement for fear of being seen as someone who wants to put women back into the dark ages and take away their rights and equality. As a woman, mother, professional, and human being, I strongly believe these negative impacts must be discussed.

As a man in today's society, have you noticed that women are now expected to get-it-all, have-it-all, and do-it-all while looking skinny, fabulous, youthful, and sexy? I strongly believe that these expectations have taken a great toll on all of us: men, women, children, and our society. Yes, women are fabulous, magnificent, and capable of accomplishing anything they set their minds to, *just* as men are. Nevertheless, handling all of these responsibilities, at the same time, lends itself to allowing parts of these very large and overwhelming tasks to suffer. Every woman experiences this challenge to some degree, but the particular part or parts of her responsibilities that are affected depend on her and her life. One woman's career may suffer. Another woman's children might pay the price. Yet another woman may lose her inner-personal life and her relationship with her man. Whichever part or parts are affected, the important factor is that legitimate suffering is occurring. In each of these areas of life: intimate relationship, home, children, career, and personal, there are specific consequences, which occur when they are not being taken care of one-hundred percent of the time.

Over the past couple of decades, women's publications

have been spoon-feeding women advice on how to "balance it all." Let us think about this one. Why are women being told over and over that they must balance it all? In addition, why have men been left out as if they are incapable of much of anything?

This attitude which states that men are incapable, inferior, stupid, and incompetent is propagated in television shows and commercials (that our children are watching), movies, and in many women's magazines.

There was a fast food commercial recently, which perfectly exemplifies these false standards. The scenario goes something like this: three guys are sitting on a couch watching football and drinking beer. After a few moments of cheering, yelling, and beer swigging, a fourth man enters the living room from the kitchen wearing an apron, oven mitts, and carrying a cooking tray of home-baked biscuits. "Anyone want biscuits?" he asks, while offering the tray. Dead silence blankets the room. His friends, no longer cheering, stare at him blank-faced with an expression that says, *Is this guy a pussy or what?* The voice-over soon interjects in a deep, stern voice, "Real men don't bake!"

These types of commercials diminish men's roles and expectations as members of our society. This commercial does more than encourage you to buy some fast food biscuits; it tells viewers that "real men" aren't supposed to like baking but *are* suppose to watch football, swig beer, and expect that only a woman should bake. Obviously, "real men" can like baking and cooking. In fact, there are very famous male chefs and bakers who are finding great success with their talent. However, for some reason, men continue to be pigeonholed into a role of the stupid, incompetent, sports-obsessed cretin. Along with this, men are also viewed as someone a woman can "learn" how to manipulate and train. These messages are a farce! Men are marketed to and emasculated, represented as so much less than who they truly are, while women are continually marketed to and told over and over they must balance it all, leaving them disappointed in themselves when they can't maintain the frenzied pace. These false, societal gender roles are an absurd double standard that do not serve anyone—men, women, or children. Why do we have these unrealistic expectations for men and women and why is no one talking about how harmful this can be for everyone in our families and our society?

I want to share with you that I have had so many female friends and clients confess to me that they are ashamed of wanting and wishing they could stay home, raise their children, and keep the home. They have shared how they feel so smothered and unhappy by the pressure of having to do it all. This guilt and shame I hear from women today, not only from my friends and from my clients, but also from women in general, is astounding.

They quite often feel that they must do it all or they are

not good enough. This is so important for you, as a man, to understand, because your awareness and understanding helps shift this paradigm, which has taken us all down a road that is not serving any of us well. Simply put, you count. You are important. You are equal and very, very vital in this big picture.

So, let us look at the big picture here.

Yes, women progressed and received the right to vote, work, attend college, and run for President of the United States. However, what price have men, women, and children had to pay for these freedoms? Take a long hard look at our society. Are you happy with what you see? Do you consider our society healthy, happy, and functioning?

When we look at today's society, we can see that the family unit and a true sense of community have broken down. Divorce is tearing families apart at an alarming rate. Children are frequently left at home alone out of necessity. People often feel isolated and lonely. Many times, even when the family stays together, both men and women are pushed to their limits and are overly stressed in order to survive financially.

We all are now in a time when an awakening needs to occur. An awakening and change for all of us: men, women, our children, and our society. We must all wake up and become conscious about what is really important to us. Discover what life is really all about and seek out our true purpose. Is this to say women should be quieted, put back in the kitchen, and encouraged to stay barefoot and pregnant or does this mean that "real men" should only be concerned with sports, their careers, and expect their women to do all the cooking and cleaning? Absolutely not! However, it does mean, each man and woman must find the inner strength to be true to him or herself. Each man and woman must know and understand what is most important and then fearlessly live from that choice. Each man and woman must set boundaries around what they want their life to be and discover how to accomplish these goals. Individually, each person must courageously find the road to fulfillment, within each of his or her own heart first. Then they can come together honestly and authentically to create a mutually fulfilled and rich life.

With that said, I would like for you now to have your personal notebook ready to answer the following questions with you and your woman specifically in mind:

> Right now, are there any areas in your life as a man or as part of a couple, which are suffering?
>
> Are you or your woman experiencing any feelings of guilt in the areas of family, career, relationship, or society?
>
> How about embarrassment?
>
> Perhaps any shame?
>
> How about stress?

On a scale from 1 to 10 (10 being stressed out completely), what stress level rating would you and your woman have right now?

How about any anxiety?

Feelings of depression?

Feelings of frustration?

Feelings of being overwhelmed?

At the end of the day, are you and your woman feeling confident about all you have accomplished in the areas of family, career, purpose, and your personal lives?

Are you left feeling unsatisfied?

If you feel unsatisfied, how would you like to see your life change?

After answering the above questions, create the painting of your perfect lifestyle using your most vivid imagination. Each of our ideal lifestyles is unique; now is the time to discover yours. Explore what would feel and be the very best life for you.

Give yourself permission. Go ahead, allow yourself to paint the picture of all your possibilities.

Remember, in your imagination, there are no rules, restrictions, and laws. Push through any blocks that might tell you, "You can't have that. It's impossible!" Push through and create this in your mind. Get a very clear picture of your perfect lifestyle.

Now, how do you create this perfect lifestyle and how does all of this relate to the simple desire a woman has to feel safe and provided for by her man?

Everything!

In my observations, most men are so confused by today's gender standards. The over-responsibility expected of women and the emasculation of men has taken your clear and well-defined roles away from you. Adding insult to injury, no instructions were given for how your behavior should be replaced or redefined. Most men do not know if they should open a woman's door, offer to pay, or expect her—the woman—to make the first move. Your father, grandfather, and great-grandfather knew exactly what was expected of them, from both women and society. Unfortunately, men today have not been given those same clear boundaries. I have heard time and time again from my male clients and friends that they just do not know what to do or how to behave as a man with a woman anymore.

In almost every situation, I believe the answer is balance. Not the type of balance as, "You have to balance it all and look great at the same time" but true inner balance.

Within each of us, we all possess both masculine and feminine qualities and energies. Learning what and how these qualities and energies interact within us is vital.

To further explain, if we look at the Ancient Eastern Cultures, there is a symbol called Tao. The belief about this symbol is based on the thought system that the Tao is a circle divided in two equal parts: Yin and Yang. Each of these parts, however, contains an element of the other, indicating that all of creation is composed of two energies held in harmony and interaction. In this belief system, the Yang energy represents the masculine and the Yin energy represents the feminine. The Yang or masculine energy is usually described as being direct, focused, logical, and action oriented. The Yin or feminine energy is usually described as intuitive, creative, and receptive. Coming into a deeper understanding of how these two energies exist within ourselves can assist us in operating from a place of inner balance.

Once we have this inner balance, then men and women can come together as a couple from a place of complementing one another rather than competing against their partners. Men and women will no longer be competing head-to-head against one another with "who is the better or stronger gender." Instead, men and women will interact together from a place of mutual honor and respect.

Up until this point, you have experienced some practice looking inwardly with many of the exercises you have completed in this book.

Now, for the next step. At this time, take your personal notebook out and answer the following questions:

What parts of you are logical, direct, focused, and action oriented?

When are these elements and energies usually expressed in your everyday life?

What parts of you are creative, intuitive, and receptive?

When are these elements and energies usually expressed in your everyday life?

Which of these parts of you do you like?

Which of these parts do you not like?

Is there any correlation between the parts you like and do not like and your feelings and thoughts about males or females?

Understanding the strengths of yourself and others helps you appreciate what each of us has to offer. There is great peace in this respectful understanding. Loving one another in this manner allows men to be men and women to be women. The balance works because each gender recognizes, appreciates, respects, and honors these gifts within themselves and in one another. Acting and feeling so allows for the natural flow of the masculine and feminine elements and energies to thrive and flourish together harmoniously.

Let us now take the information you just learned and go create your desired lifestyle in your imagination. Whatever you imagine, whether it is grandiose, simple, or somewhere in between, now is the time to open up and share your desired lifestyle with your woman, so you can achieve this lifestyle together.

To be more specific, let's say you have decided—in your ideal lifestyle—that you would like for your woman to pursue her career until you have children. At that time, she will stay home in order to raise your children. If you both agree on this plan, you then make the plan to accomplish these goals both fiscally and logistically. Perhaps you already have children and she would like to leave her job or career in order to stay home and be more present in your children's lives. Another possibility is you would like to leave work and stay home with the children, instead. Perhaps you do not want children and wish to travel the world or work for charitable causes in Africa. Whatever lifestyle you desire, the key is to work the details out with your partner, so you can see it to fruition.

When working on this part of healing, a common concern I hear from my clients is that many men and women worry it is impossible to achieve what they really want. The good news is that the truth is the very opposite. When you are clear and straightforward about your desired lifestyle with yourself and your partner and you *believe* it is possible to have it, then The Universe (*God*) aligns with what you believe can happen. Suddenly options open up and present themselves to you. If you remain true to yourself and your desires—doors, windows, and pathways will effortlessly and naturally open up for you. The key for making your ideal lifestyle come to fruition is your *belief* that it is possible and *feeling* worthy of having it.

Now let us discuss the three simple desires of a man...

I. Good food

II. Good sex with *his* woman

III. To feel that *his* woman thinks he is the greatest man in the world

Reading these desires probably makes just good common sense, right? To provide you with more clarity on the various perspectives of these desires, I will explain them in such a way that you may have a deeper understanding from a woman's perspective. By doing so, I am providing for you the necessary tools to use in your relationship with your woman and all the women in your life.

Now, for the first desire.

I. Good Food

You have probably heard the old-fashioned saying, "The way to a man's heart is through his stomach." Stop and think for a moment. Where do you think this cliché came from? Think about this—it really is simple.

What do you think food represents?

How do you feel when your stomach is full of good food?

How do you feel when your stomach is full of good food prepared by the woman you love?

How do you feel when sharing a good meal with your women?

Are you starting to put the picture together? A man *feels good* when his stomach is full with good food! He feels satisfied and content. It's that simple! We could dive into a deep, psychological discussion on this one, but it all boils down to a simple concept. A man feels good when his stomach is full of good food!

Now, don't panic if your woman has never set foot in a kitchen or burns everything she attempts to cook. There are ways around this: cooking classes, going out to eat, or calling in for delivery. You may even be a man who is the cook in your relationship and how wonderful is that?! With this first desire, it is important that your woman simply be with you. "Be" with you means to be present and share in the experience. You want your woman to be a positive part of the process of filling you up with good food. So, whether she is preparing the food, helping you prepare the food, or ordering the food in for delivery, the part to remember is *your woman* is around and part of the process. Sharing the experience is best when you and your woman approach it with a great attitude filled with love. The problem, which can arise, however, is that your woman may be so unaware of a man's desire for a good meal with his woman. She may completely not get it, understand it, or think it is important. To most men, this probably seems like a no-brainer. Of course, you want good food! The process of eating good food and the feeling of how good it is once you have eaten seems very normal. It is very normal to most men. However, to most women, this experience is more complicated.

Let me explain why.

Many women, even the most "all-together" ones have developed some sort of issue around food or their body image. I believe this is especially true in the United States, primarily due to the impossible beauty standards set by the fashion industry along with beauty-product corporations. These standards are then distributed by the major media outlets: television, movies, and magazines. From a very young age, women are continually bombarded every day to "look" a certain way. The mass media regularly "tells" women that they are <u>not</u> good enough the way they are, but if they buy a specific fashion trend, make-up application, diet aid, or surgical cosmetic improvement they just might be good enough. To add insult to injury, these negative and demeaning messages are added to by implying that men are only attracted to women and desire them if they look "this way." As intelligent, deep, and complicated as most women are, I believe many of them are missing the boat on this one. Instead of rejecting these false projections and ideas, many buy into the messages at their own expense, which then often negatively affects the man in their life.

How, you might be wondering, does this affect the man in their life?

Well, let us say that the woman in your life is not feeling good about her weight or her body—this then affects all areas of her life. If she is feeling unattractive or "fat," her thoughts, moods, attitudes, and overall state of being are negatively impacted. Simply put, she does not feel good. These internal feelings are then externally expressed through her words and actions. For example, let's say you have a date planned with your woman. You are looking forward to the time together and have no idea that she is currently "feeling fat." She begins to get ready, proceeds to her closet to pick out something to wear, and starts trying on various outfits. One outfit after another, she looks in the mirror and feeling disgusted by what she sees, rips the clothing off and throws the articles on the bed only to try again with another outfit. Ten minutes later the bed is covered in a pile of discarded clothes. She is feeling frustrated and defeated. Her thoughts are swirling around about how bad she looks and she realizes she is running out of time. She pulls herself together and begrudgingly decides on an outfit. You then walk into the room, completely unaware of any of these emotional states and tell her how beautiful she looks. You expect a simple, "Thanks Honey," but instead, she whips around and says in disgust with you, "I look fat! How could you say I look beautiful?!"

Sound familiar? Being on the receiving end of this situation is not much fun, is it?

I have had many male friends and clients share with me that this type of situation left them feeling invalidated and demeaned, as if their opinion just didn't matter that much. Each would explain how it left him feeling frustrated, angry, and defeated. The irony in this situation is that your woman wants and desires you to tell her she is beautiful. However, if she is not feeling beautiful herself first, then she can (and more than likely will) unknowingly turn those negative emotions around and project them onto you!

If we all can understand that one of the most significant ways females are directly and negatively impacted is through their weight and body, important changes in our relationships can be accomplished. The unnecessary angst women go through on a daily basis concerning their body and weight would be eliminated, which would then stop women from projecting their own negative feelings onto their men. The important thing to understand is that, unfortunately, this perspective is not found in just a few women—it is shared by most women.

Unbelievably, I have found that even most models, which are paid *because* of their looks, have issues around their body and their weight. I have personally been on several television sets and photo shoots where I witnessed this exact situation firsthand. Collectively, the models complained about how "fat" they were or how unhappy they were with their bodies. Mind you, these women were not only visually beautiful and in great shape, they were being paid quite well for exactly the way their bodies looked. Yet they all clearly and consistently expressed dislike toward their bodies.

Why am I sharing this with you?

I am not trying to make easy excuses for women, but rather help you—as a man—to gain a deeper understanding of women and more specifically, *your* woman.

We all know the common joke, "Honey, do these jeans make my butt look fat?" I believe if men and women could understand where this question—and others like it—comes from, a lot of unnecessary angst and problems within their relationship would be eliminated.

How?

Well, I have found that with almost any issue, when there is understanding, there is healing. I want to use an exaggerated example to further explain this point. As you read, try to stay open and imagine how you would feel on a daily basis and how your life would be different if this situation were a reality:

Imagine for a moment that from the time you were a very young boy you were "told" by all the major forms of media that your penis *has* to be twelve inches long and four inches thick. Every day, you are constantly bombarded with the message that unless you have a 12" x 4" penis you are just not good enough in any manner. Now, imagine that you see this message in everything you do. If you watch television, go see a movie, read a magazine, notice an ad on the side of a bus, or read billboards as you drive—literally anywhere you go or anything you do—you see the insinuated message, *Women will only want and desire you if you have a twelve inch by four inch penis!*

Can you imagine how awful and damaging this would be for you and your self-worth? Can you imagine how this would impact all aspects of your life? Now, let us imagine that you have an average size penis. Yet, you are constantly feeling inadequate because of the societal expectation that a "real man is larger." You feel as if you must "do" something to get your penis up to par. Now, imagine that there is a trillion-dollar industry solely dedicated to making, producing, marketing, and selling products to increase the size of your penis or at least to make your penis "appear" larger.

How would you feel?

What would you think?

How would this impact your life?

I know this may sound like a ridiculous and unbelievable example, but I hope it puts into perspective the massive manipulation of girls and women in this country.

I believe that if men were marketed to on such a scale, they would rise up against such nonsense and disregard it as ludicrous. Women, on the other hand, have not fully risen up against this ridiculousness. Rather, they have bought into it hook, line, and sinker. Women that is most women—and more likely than not *your* woman—constantly go through this internal angst of not being good enough, especially in terms of their body and weight.

Now, in order to gain a truly full-rounded perspective, let's flip this around a little and talk about some of the ways in which men, maybe even you, are affected by a similar societal dynamic. Let us talk about this, in regards to a man's height, his hairline, and his financial status. Quite often, these are the exact aspects that men are judged upon and then placed into a particular category of "value" or "worth." Let me ask you, what do you think some of the first questions a woman will ask a friend when she is being set up on a blind date? Her questions will usually sound something like:

"How tall is he?"

"What does he do for a living?"

"Does he have his hair or is he balding?"

These standards of value and worth *do* exist for men in our country and are just as unfair as the ones placed on women. Are they as overtly obvious? No! As I mentioned before, I believe men would rise up and rebel against the absurd superficial standards women still accept. However, these "messages" of value and worth placed upon men *are* out there and *do* exist.

According to these societal standards, a man's "worth" and "value" are proportionately contingent upon how he measures up in these areas.

For example:

Let us look at two different men. We will start with man A, whom we will call Ken. Ken is 6'4" tall, with a full head of hair, and makes a "good living." Now we will meet man B, whom we will call Tim. Tim is 5'6" tall, balding, and he is "just getting by" financially. According to our society, which one do you believe is judged instantly to have more "value" or "worth?"

Now, let us further get to know who these men really are. With Ken, once you got to know him, you would discover that he is a guy that blows off his friends when they are in need, cheats on every woman he is ever with, and is ruthless and dishonest in his business dealings. Whereas with Tim, once you got to know him, you would discover he is one of the most loyal friends you could ever want to have, is an honorable man in his relationships with women and in his business dealings, and volunteers at the local homeless shelter every week.

Now, knowing these details, which man do you believe is judged to have more "value" and "worth?"

In our society, why are men immediately judged on these aspects?

Why is it that a man receives instant regard when he is financially successful, even if he is ruthless and unethical?

Why are men considered "less than" if they lose their hair?

Why are men most often judged and categorized, especially by women, by such shallow and superficial aspects?

To be a man in today's world is not easy.

The days of a once clearly defined model of what a "good man" is are long gone. Today, men are bombarded by "strong and aggressive" women in the workforce and at home, who often knowingly and unknowingly emasculate them. At the same time, they are frequently conveyed in the media as being stupid, insensitive, incapable, and "manly." Men are no longer respected the way they once were; nor are they viewed the way they once were. I believe men got the royal shaft through the women's rights movement and no one has stopped to turn around and help clean up the mess! I say a "mess" because that is what it has turned into, for all of us.

We need men to be allowed to be men.

Each man should have the right to become the best and greatest man he can be. When a man is allowed this freedom of personal expression, he is given the opportunity to mature into what it really means to be a "good man." When this opportunity occurs, he can then positively affect the members of his family, his woman, his children, his friends, his co-workers, his community, generations to come, and the world.

So, let's talk a little about what it means to be a "good man." When you hear those words, what comes to mind?

The definition of what makes a man into a "good man" is up to each and every man for himself.

We could assign certain characteristics such as: honest, kind, strong, capable, loyal, hard working, good provider, giving, diligent, forgiving, leader, loving, faith-filled, fair, thoughtful, and honorable. However, each man must define for himself what exactly this means for him.

In looking at how this is reflected in your own life, you then have the opportunity to become your exact definition of a "good man." Your life can then be a living example of exactly what a good man is. By being true to yourself, instead of the societal standards placed upon you, you can leave this world better than how you found it and help make everyone you touch in your life better for knowing you.

How do you feel as you read these words?

Have you ever thought about what it means for you to be a "good man"?

If in this very moment, you take a look at who you are today and what your life expresses to yourself and those around you; how do you feel you are doing with it all?

What areas of yourself would you like to further develop?

What areas do you feel really good about?

Who are you today as a man?

Who would you like to become as a man?

The concept we have been talking about is really very simple: each gender is negatively impacted in one way or another by certain societal standards and expectations, which then can negatively affect our relationships with one another and ourselves. Therefore, if we could all get to a place of understanding, empathy, and compassion for one another and ourselves—our lives and our relationships would be much richer and more fulfilled. For example, the next time your woman asks you, "Honey, do I look fat in this?" you have the amazing opportunity to look her in the eye with your new understanding and say to her, "You are the most beautiful woman in the world to me! You look so beautiful all the time...I always want you!" At the same time, your woman has the same opportunity to love and support you in the ways, which best serve you.

Let's visit again the first simple desire we began discussing: a man's desire for good food. Now that you have a deeper understanding of women and the issues most of them have around their weight and bodies, you can approach your woman from this place of understanding. You can simply share with her your newfound perspective. Then, you can help her understand that having her involved with you and filling your body with good food feels good! Once a woman understands this, it makes it a whole lot easier for her to show up for you in this way. As well, once you have a perspective on how societal standards affects both genders, you can also have a deeper understanding as to how this is impacting your relationship with yourself, your woman, and the experiences you share together. Remember, the more you know and communicate with one another, the better able both of you are to fulfill each other's desires. In the successful healing and nurturing of your relationship with your woman, this can become some of the most powerful "food" of all!

II. Good Sex with *His* Woman

The next simple desire is good sex. Again, this might seem beyond obvious and simply good common sense for most men. However, for most women, this one can usually trigger a whole bag of issues. The issue of sex can actually frighten or intimidate some women.

For men it is simple—you want good sex. I have found in my work that when a man has committed himself to an intimate relationship, he wants to have sex with *his* woman. This is not to say that you will not have thoughts about other women or that you will lose the primal, innate desire to spread your seed. This biological part of you is there and it has nothing to do with your love for your woman. Most of the time, a man in love and committed to his partner wants to share himself with his woman and wants his woman to desire and share herself with him. I have heard so many men report they feel awful when they know their wife or girlfriend is "just doing it" for them. Sex out of obligation can be hurtful and a huge turn off emotionally and sexually.

On the other hand, one of the greatest pleasures a man can feel—besides the actually physical pleasure from sex—is when his woman is receiving great sexual pleasure from him. In other words, when you experience her sexually responding fully to you, you feel good. You feel like a man. You feel like you are accomplishing something great! You feel as if you are taking care of your woman. This is where this simple desire of good sex really comes into play. A man feels good with good sex both physically and emotionally!

Sex is a basic, healthy, and instinctual need for all of us. However, most men and women want and desire sex in different ways. These differing desires are where many misunderstandings can occur between men and women.

The definition of "good sex" is both personal and subjective. One person may consider fifteen minutes in the missionary position to be good sex. Another person may feel an hour of passionate lovemaking is good sex. Yet others may feel that any type of sex when they have an orgasm is good sex. Many times, when addressing the sexual relationship with their partners, I hear women report they feel "used" or "like a piece of meat." They feel their man would not care who it was he was having sex with, just as long as he was "getting laid." Did you notice the word "getting" in the "getting laid?" For most women, feeling as if their partner is focused on "getting laid," can often result in feelings of anger, resentment, or being turned off completely. As a result, these feelings can lead a woman to avoid sexual intimacy, physically and emotionally pull away, or even verbally snap at her partner.

By far, the very best way to know for sure what good sex

means for you and your partner is to communicate and acknowledge each of your wants and desires. Ask her what she likes and considers good sex to be. At the same time, let her know what makes sex good for you. Discussing together what she enjoys and what you enjoy often opens the doors to wonderful and eye-opening conversations.

To help facilitate understanding of these differences and issues around sex, I want you to pull out your personal notebook and get ready for the next exercise.

On the pages to follow, you will read one word per page. During this exercise, practice being consciously aware and acting as the objective observer of you, while paying attention to the reactions of your inner child. As you read each word, stop, and give yourself at least a few minutes between pages. Pay particular attention to the thoughts entering your mind. Also, stay aware of how you feel while you read each word. Notice any reactions you may feel in your body. Stay aware and tune in to You. Once you have read each word, record in your notebook any thoughts, ideas, or feelings, which may arise for you. They can be pleasant, positive, happy, or just the opposite. Whatever the thoughts or feelings, just stay in the objective observer position and record what comes up for you.

Here we go:

F***ING

SEX

[redacted]

MAKING LOVE

This "sexual terms" exercise has the potential to bring to your awareness the various relationships you might have with sex. You might not have realized that you identify different feelings with different acts of sex. Knowing these minute, often emotional differences, can help you not only have a better understanding of your own relationship with sex, but provide you with tools for comparing your definitions with those of your partner. By discovering both the differences and similarities you share in your sexual relationship, you will begin the path of understanding how each of you feels loved and turned on during sex.

Sometimes a woman may not know how to reciprocate the type of sex you desire. Alternately, you may not know how to communicate with her about how sex is good for you. Perhaps talking about this topic with her is very uncomfortable for you. If so, you are not alone, as this is a common trap for many couples. Many times, one or both partners feel that if they try to tell their partner what they like, they will somehow insult them or hurt their feelings. The irony of this is that most men and women *do* want their partners to tell them how to sexually please them. I have found that men, especially, are very eager to understand what their women want in bed.

In general, the human body is sexually stimulated pretty much all in the same way. For example, touching a woman's clitoris or stroking a man's penis will bring about sexual arousal. However, the specifics of how someone, man or woman, feels most stimulated is unique to each man or woman. Do you remember the general rule of thumb we discussed earlier? The one that states: most people give pleasure physically in the manner they actually want to receive physically? For example, if a woman likes soft, repetitive, light, tickling touches, that is often the way she will touch her partner. On the other hand, if a man likes strong, deep rubs, then that is often the way he will touch his partner. Think about that for a moment and try to figure out what type of physical touch you give to your partner. Now ask yourself, *Is this the type of physical touch I like to receive*? This is also very enlightening to do with your partner. Ask her the same questions and see what you discover together. Simply becoming aware of this general rule of thumb can help you and your partner start communicating and understanding one another's sexual desires.

Another good rule of thumb for sexually pleasing your woman is to understand and remember the following key ingredients. Most women want to feel emotionally and physically turned on *before* having sex. What does this mean exactly? It's simple—let us start with the emotional part. Your woman wants to *feel* connected to you emotionally before she takes off her clothes. This means she wants to feel heard (which we will fully discuss in the next chapter), desired, and truly loved by you. If your woman feels this from you, moving to the next step, being physically turned on, is much easier. Now, that is not to say women cannot ever have impulsive, spur-of-the-moment sex. Again, every person's comfort level and approach to sex can be different. As a general guideline, however, women are more emotionally driven in the initiation of sex than are men. Therefore, learning these little differences can help you understand why your woman may or may not respond to your sexual invitations.

The most common mistake a man makes when initiating sex with his woman is "bottom-lining" it. Now, this approach may be good for you in your life, your work, and the way you best communicate. However, when it comes to sex with your woman, you will need to throw this approach out the window.

To help you understand this perspective, I would like you to think of your woman's body as a perfectly tuned and maintained sports car. Now, imagine that you want to take this sports car out for a little pleasure spin. Imagine that as you press down on the gas pedal intending to go from 0 – 60 mph in five seconds flat, you discover your beloved sports car has no oil or gas in it. In fact, your sports car—as beautiful as it is—is completely dry of any fluids. What would you do? Well, I am hoping you would fill the car with gas, oil, and all the necessary fluids before taking off next time—right? Great! Surprisingly, it is the same thing with your woman's body. She needs the necessary fluids in check in order to go fast. She usually gets these "fluids," when she is emotionally connected with you and when you put the time into foreplay with her—making her entire body, not just her breast and vagina, an important aspect of sex. Her sensations will be heightened and her body will have had the time to become lubricated. Really, turning a woman on is that simple.

Now, how *your* woman specifically becomes "lubricated" is unique to her. If you do not know how she is turned on, your job is to ask and find out. Simply ask her what makes her sexually stimulated, so she may share with you what she likes, what turns her on, and gets her juices flowing.

To help understand this concept further, let's look at it in action—remember George and Trudy?

They have each committed to doing their own inner work. They have built and are maintaining a healthy relationship with themselves and their inner children. They are now ready to start working on their intimate relationship. As they do so, they start with attempting to talk about their sex life.

Let's listen:

George, who is feeling very uncomfortable and shy about Trudy and he discussing their sex life says, "Trudy, Honey...can we talk about our sex life...is that okay with you?"

Trudy, feeling shocked by this request and a little nervous about what he is going to tell her says, "Sure! Just as long as you don't tell me we have to have it three times a day!"

George replies, "No, Honey, unless you wanted to do it three times a day, in which case, I would be delighted to accommodate you! What I really want to talk about and ask is...well...how do you get your fluids flowing? Wait a minute that is not what I meant...what I mean is how do you like to be turned on before we have sex?"

Trudy, now delighted that George is taking the time to ask and find out what works for her says, "Well, usually you grab at my breasts to get things going...and...well...you see...I don't like it...what I mean is...it doesn't feel good to me."

George is shocked by this comment and replies, "Wow, Honey! I never knew that bothered you! I thought you liked it because I was showing you I was interested and desired you. Do you ever like when I touch your breasts?"

Feeling a bit more confident, Trudy replies, "Yes! I really like it when you kiss them softly while we are making love."

George, becoming aroused by the very thought says, "Gee, Honey. I love to kiss your breasts. What else do you like? How do you want me to start sex? I really want to know."

And so begins the path of understanding one another's road map to a healthy sexual relationship: asking each other what you enjoy, listening to one another, and then sharing in the experience together.

It's that simple. Good sex feels good for *both* partners!

III. To Feel that *His* Woman Thinks He is The Greatest Man in the World

Now, for the third simple desire a man wants in his intimate relationship: to feel as if his woman thinks he is the greatest man in the world.

What does that mean exactly?

Simply, a man wants to feel that his woman believes he is the "Man of all men."

Would most men admit this to themselves or their woman? Probably not. However, if you look inwardly and at the other men you might know in your life, it will probably be revealed that men like to feel admired, respected, and adored by their women.

Frequently, my male friends and clients have said, while talking about the woman in their life, "It is just the way she looks at me. I know she loves me!"

Men love this—to be with a woman who is confident in him and respects him for who he is as a person. Most men want to feel that who they are and what they can provide is good enough.

However, what I hear more often from my male friends and male clients are stories about how their women try changing them to make them "better." Often, these accounts are filled with all the ways the woman tells him exactly what is wrong with him and how he should be instead. I want you to stop in this moment and ask yourself the following two questions:

1. Does this happen in my relationship?
2. How do I feel, if I am frequently told how wrong I am and how I could be better?

These questions are very important, because they provide you with the opportunity to look at your self-worth within your relationship.

By nature, most women are "caretakers," "fixers," "doers," and are able to multitask during it all. In addition, most women are very comfortable running the show and taking care of what needs to be done. Such traits are wonderful to have in the work force, while running a business, raising children, or running a household. However, "running the show" is not always such a great thing when it spills over into our intimate relationships and how you are being treated as a man. You see, when your woman consistently tells you how wrong you are or that how you are doing something is incorrect, I doubt you feel like a man, or her equal. Instead, you probably end up feeling beaten down. Most men, when feeling like this, will withdraw and go into their "cave."

Does this sound familiar?

If so, it's okay. This seclusion is a natural self-protection. You want to tune out the negative messages and get back to a place where you are not feeling so badly.

So, why does this dynamic occur so often with so many women?

My answer is: **unawareness**.

Most of the time, a woman is not trying to make her man feel like less than a man, she is just trying to fix the situation. Women believe that if they can fix you, they can fix what is wrong in the relationship and it will all be better. Oh, but how this backfires! A woman "fixing" her partner is not the course of action to take, for the effort is fruitless and does nothing but cause pain and damage in the relationship. The more fruitful course of action is for her to figure out what really is bothering her. She can do this by going inwardly and asking, *Where is this really coming from*? This allows her to have the ability to gain a personal perspective. The next step is for her to communicate with you about the issue in a way that does not beat you down. For example, let us say you are consistently late, consequently causing her to run late. When this scenario happens, she feels so annoyed, angry, and upset that she will yell at you, scold you, or give you the cold shoulder with disgust written all over her face. She reacts to the situation instead of dealing with her feelings. When a scenario like this occurs, ask yourself, *Where is this anger really coming from?* As well, she should ask herself the same question. When we open up to discover what the anger is really about, instead of reacting to the situation, we begin to address the anger directly. *What is the anger really about?* After asking this question, perhaps you both discover that she is really feeling disrespected and unimportant. From here, she thinks back to when she can remember feeling this way in childhood. Perhaps she discovers that, as a child, she often was left feeling this way around her mother. Situations were always about her mother and her mother's needs, leaving her feeling pushed aside without regard to her needs or feelings.

Ah-Ha! You have something here!

Now, in this moment, is when she would go in and work with her inner child on this exact issue.

Perhaps, you discover that you are reacting to your woman in a certain manner that was caused by your childhood. Possibly, you discover that when you were little, your desires and wishes were never taken seriously. So, as an adult, you make sure your needs are taken care of first without regard to your partner or anyone else around you.

Ah-Ha! You now have another piece of valuable information.

Once this newfound awareness is applied, both of you will have the opportunity to create a positive shift. You will no longer be easily triggered and have the same emotional reaction to the situation.

So back to the simple desire of feeling that your woman thinks you are the greatest man in the world. How does she communicate this to you and not try to change you?

Simple. She looks at you with eyes of compassion and love. This must begin with herself first. She must accept, honor, and love **ALL** of herself. From here, she simply turns to you and does the very same. She accepts, honors, and loves **ALL** of you—all the amazing wonder of you, your wounds, unhealed places, and your inner child—embracing it all. At the same time, she sees that you are not out to get her, hurt her, or upset her on purpose. She understands that you are just as dear, tender, and fragile in certain places as is she.

Being able to apply this understanding with yourself and your partner is such a beautiful and healing gift. This gift can be given in all areas of your life and with all the different relationships in your life. This gift brings with it such sweet peace, kindness, and love to you and all those who are in your life.

6 COMMUNICATION IS KEY

"Wise men talk because they have something to say; fools because they have to say something."

Plato, Greek Philosopher (427 – 347 BC)

Knowing and understanding the simple desires of a man or a woman is one thing. Being able to communicate about these desires effectively is another.

Healthy and loving communication is absolutely vital in all relationships, including the one with ourselves. The ability to convey to another person exactly what you are thinking and feeling is an amazing gift. Some of the most successful people in the world owe their achievements to a natural ability to effectively communicate.

For those of us who were not born with the natural gift of effective communication, we can learn a few simple techniques to put in our toolbox, which will assist in the process of learning this skill.

Whomever you are trying to communicate with, whether it is your mother, father, brother, sister, friend, co-worker, boss, stranger, child, or partner, the first communication technique for your toolbox is: *clarity.*

You must have clarity on exactly what it is you would like your listener to hear. Men generally have an easier time with this tool. For many women, however, this step can be a bit difficult, simply because of the way women think and process information. Many times, when a woman is upset about something or is just not sure what it is she is trying to say, she will talk until the message naturally comes out. The actual process of talking offers the avenue to clarity, which she needs to relay an effective message. The conversation provides her with the ability to gain some understanding.

For example, let's consider a woman we will call Sue:

Sue had a very bad day and is heading home. She knows when she arrives home, she will make dinner, pay bills, help her kids with their homework, clean up, do some laundry, and the list goes on. All of a sudden, Sue feels a wave of anxiety come over her but is not quite sure why. She calls a girlfriend and starts talking to her without a particular direction in mind. As she is sharing with her friend and releasing her emotions, Sue realizes she is overwhelmed by all the responsibilities on her shoulders. Furthermore, she recognizes that she is feeling resentful towards her husband, Bill, for not sharing in the family's responsibilities. Now that she has sorted out her thoughts through her conversation, Sue has the clarity she needs to speak with Bill.

Before we learn how Sue can successfully communicate with her partner, I want you to imagine the scene between Sue and Bill if she had not talked through her emotions with her girlfriend.

Without the clarity and insight into her resentful feelings:

Sue enters her home and starts talking about everything to Bill until she gains some understanding about what is really bothering her. Meanwhile, Bill, who has had his own long day, hears what she is saying as nagging, or white noise he has to tolerate. He immediately becomes disinterested and maybe even defensive. Sue then sees this response in him, even if he has not said a word, and acts out emotionally either through yelling, blaming, shaming, or giving the silent treatment. Now on the defense with one another, Sue and Bill start fighting about why he can't be sensitive to her needs and why she can't ever be happy with him, no matter what he does. During this time, the kids are overhearing their parents' argument from the living room and they begin to worry if everything is okay. One unfocused, blithering conversation resulted in Sue, Bill, and their children all feeling upset.

This is not a positive outcome for Bill, Sue, and their family and certainly not what Sue intended to happen when she arrived home.

Now, let's explore the conversation differently. After

speaking with her girlfriend on the way home, imagine Sue is starting with perfect clarity as to what she wants her listener, Bill, to hear. Sue enters her home and asks Bill if she can speak with him when he has a few moments. He nods his head, saying there are a few things he needs to do first. She agrees and moves on with her evening. A few hours later, Bill lets Sue know he is available to talk.

Now that you understand and are ready to implement the skill of having clarity on exactly what you would like your listener to hear, you are ready to employ the next technique for your toolbox: *style of delivery*.

The actual style of delivery for men and women is different. Most men like and respond well to messages provided in a short, clear, and concise manner. Most women like and respond well when they have room within a conversation to process the information and their emotional response.

Let us start with two different examples.

Example 1:

"Honey," begins Sue, "While I was driving home tonight, I was thinking about our lives, the kids, the house, and my job. Did I tell you what my boss did today? Ugh! That man makes me crazy. Anyway, little Sue has a dance recital next week. I have to get her costume picked up, I have to get Billy to the doctor for that earache he has been having, the housework has been piling up for over a week now, and I am feeling so bad about it all! I don't think I can do it all anymore! I mean, nothing is getting done around the house, the kids need me, and I just can't do it. I feel so bad all the time, like I'm failing and I don't know what to do!"

Example 2:

"Honey," begins Sue, "Thanks for taking the time to listen to me. I am feeling very overwhelmed by all the responsibilities of our family and my job. I need some help."

Can you see the difference here?

How do you suppose Bill will respond to Sue in Example 1? Can you see all the flowery language around the true message she is trying to convey? Can you see that in Example 2, Bill will have an easier time distinguishing the exact message she is trying to convey?

By succinctly communicating her message, Sue opens the conversation with a clear, concise, and simple request. Bill does not need to navigate through all her feelings and thoughts to figure out what she wants him to hear. This process is easy for him. Now he can discuss with her exactly what they can do together to remedy the situation. Once they do, Sue and Bill will walk away from the conversation feeling great, instead of confused, angry, or beaten up.

When a man is speaking with a woman, his delivery must provide space in the conversation so she can process the information he is sharing and her feelings. This is especially true if he is sharing something she is unaware of or not sure about. This need for processing information has nothing to do with a woman's intelligence level. Rather, it is simply how many women process unclear or new information.

Now let us look at two additional examples.

Example 1:

"Honey," begins Sue, "While I was driving home tonight, I was thinking about our lives, the kids, the house, and my job. Did I tell you what my boss did today? Ugh! That man makes me crazy. Anyway, little Sue has a dance recital next week. I have to get her costume picked up, I have to get Billy to the doctor for that earache he has been having, the housework has been piling up for over a week now, and I am feeling so bad about it all! I don't think I can do it all anymore! I mean, nothing is getting done around the house, the kids need me, and I just can't do it. I feel so bad all the time, like I'm failing and I don't know what to do!"

Bill, who does not understand a woman's need to process information and her feelings responds, "Sue, what in the hell are you talking about?!"

Example 2:

Bill who is fully aware of his woman's need to process information and her feelings says, "Sue, Honey, it sounds as if you're going through and feeling a lot."

Can you see how in Example 2, Bill opens the conversation up for Sue to keep processing her feelings?

This response allows her the opportunity to gain her own clarity. Responsive interaction occurs because he is validating her feelings and providing a space in which she can continue sharing with him. Meanwhile, his first response, "Sue, what in the hell are you talking about?!" would most likely shut down the conversation and may cause hurt feelings.

Now, let's flip this example around a little. In the next scenario, Bill has something to say to Sue.

Let's listen...

"Sue, Honey, I need to talk to you about our money

situation."

Immediately fearful that Bill is going to lecture her about money, Sue replies, "I told you we needed those new items for the house—I'm not spending too much money. You have no idea how much these things cost!"

Recognizing that Sue is already on the defensive, Bill responds calmly and patiently, knowing that this one is going to take awhile! "Honey, I wasn't going to tell you you're spending too much money. Do you feel I tell you that a lot?"

Sue, relieved that she is not in for another lecture says, "Yes, actually, I feel like you're on me all the time about it."

Bill has been focusing on his inner work, so he calmly replies, "Oh Honey, I never want you to feel that way. That is never my intention. I didn't realize you felt like this. Can you tell me how I could talk to you about my concerns without you feeling that I am attacking you about it?"

Sue, now feeling the space and freedom to process her thoughts and emotions replies, "Really, you never knew? Well, when you walk right up to me and start showing me the credit card bills and telling me I can't do this anymore, I can't stand it! I feel like you're trying to control me. I feel like you don't understand how much things really cost these days and are just blaming me for buying things we need for us or the kids or the house. It's not like I'm out there shopping for designer clothes or shoes for myself. I know we have to watch what we spend. I am not a child you know!"

Really hearing what Sue has just revealed to him, Bill replies, "Ok, I hear that you don't like when I confront you with the credit card bills and you feel that I am blaming you for buying things we need and that I am not treating you like an equal partner."

"YES!" replies Sue, thrilled that Bill truly listened to her answers. "I want to feel that you respect me and my opinions about our finances."

"I want you to know that I really do respect and value your thoughts and opinions about our money situation," responds Bill. "Can we sit down and go over it all, together?" Bill asks.

"Of course we can," she responds lovingly. "You know what Bill? I didn't even know that I felt you were treating me like a child! I'm glad we talked about this!"

I know this scenario might seem a little "too much" or far-fetched. Conversations do not always follow this flow. Sometimes, one or both of you will get angry, defensive, and want to storm away. As well, sometimes staying level headed when your woman is emotionally projecting can be very difficult to do. However, if you try the approach of truly talking through your concerns from a place of clarity, with the proper style of delivery, you will be amazed at the positive results you will witness.

Okay.

In exploring effective communication, we have discussed the importance of having clarity in the message and the proper delivery style.

The next technique for your toolbox involves: *active listening skills*.

In order to actively participate in healthy and loving communication, your listening skills must be turned on. To be more specific, listening effectively involves focusing on and understanding the actual message the speaker wants you to hear. Strong listening skills include: eye contact, observing body language, and remaining open to the other person's perspective.

While communicating, allow yourself to remain open by simply listening without preparing a preemptive response to what you think the other person is trying to tell you. Not judging a conversation is easy to do once you get the hang of it, especially if the conversation is about a neutral subject, such as baseball scores or the grocery list. This exercise can become more difficult once the conversation is emotionally charged and triggering a defensive response from you or your listener.

The word "trigger" can be described as when someone

has an emotionally charged reaction to another's words or behaviors, which is incongruent with those words or behaviors. In other words, when the action (what someone does or says) and the reaction (the response) are disproportionate or mismatched.

Let's take a look at an example of a trigger reaction from Bill:

"Honey," begins Sue, "Thanks for taking the time to listen to me. I am feeling very overwhelmed by all the responsibilities of our family and my job. I need some help."

"What?!" exclaims Bill. "You need help? What about me? God! You're just like my mother. You're never satisfied with anything I do. I can never do things right for you, can I?"

Can you hear the incongruence in this exchange? With the knowledge you have attained thus far, can you detect what is really going on here? While Sue's statement is certainly not implying Bill can never do things right for her, he hears this attack because he has been emotionally triggered. When you or someone else is triggered, it is almost as if a giant, red arrow is pointing to a wound, which has not yet healed. In the previous example, Bill obviously has been carrying around a childhood wound about never being able to please his mother.

When he hears Sue's plea for help, instead of openly listening to her, he immediately projects his own issues onto Sue without even realizing what he is doing.

At this point, their exchange can go one of two ways:

In response 1, Sue has her own emotional reaction to Bill's defensiveness, thus escalating the conversation.

In response 2, Sue remains calm, hears the true message Bill is conveying and then repeats it back to him with love.

Response 1:

Sue interjects, "How dare you compare me to your mother! I'm nothing like that woman! Maybe if you did something around here once in a while I'd be satisfied!"

Response 2:

Sue replies, "Honey, I hear that you feel you could never satisfy your mother."

Can you see how profoundly different each response is? Can you imagine how different the outcome would be to both of these responses? Response 1 would inevitably provoke further hurt and anger for both Sue and Bill. Response 2 would open the door to healing.

Effective communication all boils down to one simple concept: Would you like to be right, or would you like to be happy? When we insist on being right, positive communication rarely occurs. In fact, most of the time the discussion becomes a power struggle with each person insisting:

I'm right!

No, I'm right!

However, when we really *listen* and *hear* someone, especially someone we love, we are privy to vital information about the individual. Hearing and understanding this information gives us a great opportunity to lovingly share the knowledge. By doing so, we allow the other individual the opportunity to see wounds he or she is in need of healing. When we reflect this vital information back to our loved one, we do so without judgment, condemnation, demands, guilt, or shame. This type of caring communication simply asks you to repeat back to someone the emotional triggers you have heard.

Let's look at Sue and Bill again and explore both unloving and loving responses:

Sue's Unloving Response:

"God, Bill! When are you going to get over your mother issues? You're forty-four years old. Let it go already!"

Sue's Loving Response:

"Honey, I'm hearing you express feelings about never being able to satisfy your mother."

Just as we have the opportunity to lovingly reflect back vital information to others, we have the same opportunity to do so for ourselves. As you make use of being consciously aware and acting as the objective observer of you, you will have the same opportunity to recognize the giant, red arrows pointing to any unhealed places within you.

Let us now use Bill as an example:

Imagine Bill is actively doing his inner work and using his tools on a daily basis. As he listens to Sue ranting on and on about her issues, Bill recognizes his desire to tell her off. However, since he is diligently using his tools to grow, Bill refrains from this emotional trigger and instead, quietly processes why he feels the negative reaction. By looking inwardly, Bill realizes he is feeling just like he did every time he tried really hard to please his mother when he was a little boy. He remembers that, as a boy, he felt she would never appreciate his efforts. He could never satisfy his mother no matter how hard he tried. Now, upon this reflection, Bill is able to recognize that he is triggered and it is not actually Sue making him react this way. He knows it is his responsibility to take care of his wounded inner child. He also realizes that yelling back at Sue is fruitless. Instead, he must address his own wounds within himself and with his inner child. At this point, Bill also has a great gift to provide Sue.

Let's listen:

"Honey," responds Bill, "As you were sharing, I felt myself triggered. It is my own issue with my mother. I want to hear you and provide for you what I can. Before I'm fully able to do so, I really need a little time to work on this issue so it is not directed at you."

Wow!

How great does that sound?

Can you imagine how wonderful this would be? Having a relationship in which both partners take full responsibility for themselves, their issues, and their own personal healing—all the while honoring each other?

This healing, support, and communication is what we are all being called to bring forth in our relationships and ourselves—and it all begins with the relationship we form with ourselves.

7

YOUR AUTHENTIC SELF

"To be yourself in a world that is constantly trying to make you something else is the greatest accomplishment."

Ralph Waldo Emerson, American essayist, philosopher, poet (1803 – 1882)

We have discussed the importance of gaining self-awareness, self-acceptance, and self-love. Now it is time to give attention to what I like to call the authentic self. The authentic self is who you are, genuinely. It is your original, true, real, sincere, honest, candid, direct, actual, unique, and trustworthy self. The authentic self is not our social face, nor is it any of the masks we may wear out of fear or insecurity. It is who we truly are, without any apologies.

Being and living from your authentic self means being true to your desires, dreams, values, and most of all to yourself. There is no greater betrayal than to betray ourselves and when we deny who we truly are; this is exactly what is happening. William Shakespeare expressed it best when he wrote, "To thine own self be true." When we betray ourselves, we violate our own inner core. Standing up and being your authentic self takes a great deal of courage.

Today, it is very easy to conform to the homogenized ways of society by following the pack and not standing out from the crowd. On the contrary, it takes people with great depth of character to remain true to themselves through it all, the good times and the bad times. In fact, a person's true character is most exposed when facing life's challenges. To remain your authentic self, especially during your most vulnerable and difficult of times, is one of the greatest achievements of all.

Why do you suppose being and living from your authentic self is so significant?

By living authentically, you can recognize the magnificent, beautiful, amazing human being you are, who has the ability to bring something unique and wonderful to the world. This ability can only be expressed and shared when you are being and living from your authentic self. By living and being unafraid and unencumbered by self-doubt, you are free to be all you are meant to be.

You have a very special purpose with unique gifts that only you can bring and share in this life. You are the only one of You. The world benefits when you show up as your authentic self. From this place, you are literally co-creating that which you came here to do and share. It does not matter what "that" is. It does not matter how big or small, how locally or globally your authentic self drives you to act or live. It does not even matter if your ability helps one person or a billion people. What does matter, however, is that you are honestly able to be who you truly are.

By being your authentic self, all your uniqueness and beauty will allow your contribution to the world to be realized.

So, who is your authentic self?

The following questions are designed specifically to help you begin to discover your authentic self. I recommend doing this exercise in a quiet space with your pen and personal notebook in hand. If you get tired or overwhelmed, take a break. However, answering every question is very important in this exercise. As you have done in previous exercises, take this very slowly. Breathe between each question. Be real with yourself. Allow yourself to go within to find *your* true answers. In addition, while doing this exercise, use the tools of being consciously aware and acting as the objective observer of you. Look past all of what you have been told, taught, or conditioned to believe and think during the course of your life. Instead, answer each and every question from within you, the authentic you:

What is MY favorite color?

What is MY favorite time of year?

What is MY favorite food?

What is MY favorite time of the day?

What is MY favorite room in my house?

What is MY favorite activity?

What is MY favorite animal?

What is MY favorite book?

What is MY favorite movie?

What is MY favorite treasure?

What is MY favorite scent?

What is MY favorite part of nature?

What is MY favorite type of art?

What is MY favorite city?

What is MY favorite sport?

What is MY favorite thing to do during my down time?

What is MY favorite dessert?

What is MY favorite type of clothing to wear?

What is MY favorite weather?

When am I most hungry?

When am I tired?

When do I want to be touched?

When am I playful?

When am I at my best?

When am I usually in the mood for sex?

When am I angry?

When am I moody?

When do I feel like giving up?

When do I feel strong?

When do I feel most happy?

When do I get cranky?

When do I get excited?

When do I feel like talking?

When do I feel like being quiet?

When do I feel inspired or motivated?

When do I feel lazy?

When do I smile?

When do I feel like accomplishing my goals?

Do I like when it rains?

Do I like to laugh?

Do I like the beach?

Do I like sports?

Do I like my boss?

Do I like to be serious?

Do I like children?

Do I like to watch television?

Do I like the mountains?

Do I like my job and/or career?

Do I like my home?

Do I like spending time with my family members?

Do I like my Mom?

Do I like my Dad?

Do I like my siblings?

Do I like the way I dress?

Do I like the way I am living my life?

Do I like most people?

Do I like my partner?

How do I FEEL about my family?

How do I FEEL about trees?

How do I FEEL about my first love?

How do I FEEL about religion?

How do I FEEL about my partner?

How do I FEEL about politics?

How do I FEEL about the meaning of life?

How do I FEEL about education?

How do I FEEL about the poor?

How do I FEEL about charities?

How do I FEEL about God?

How do I FEEL about my economic state?

How do I FEEL about the rich?

How do I FEEL when I view art?

How do I FEEL when I listen to music?

How do I FEEL when I see a good movie?

How do I FEEL when I eat ice cream?

How do I FEEL when the sky is blue?

How do I FEEL about me?

What part of me do I like the best?

What part of me do I like the least?

What part of me am I afraid of?

What part of me do I celebrate?

What part of me do I hide from the world?

What part of me is delightful?

What part of me likes to sing?

What part of me likes to dance?

What part of me am I most proud of?

What part of me am I most ashamed of?

What part of me do I show off?

What part of me do I let people see?

What part of me do I know I want to change?

What part of me do I wish were different right now?

What part of me likes to play?

What part of me likes adventure?

What part of me likes to stay home?

What part of me likes to meet new people?

What part of me likes to get under the covers and hide?

What part of me believes in myself?

When I was a child, when was I most happy?

When I was a child, when was I most afraid?

When I was a child, what did I want to be?

When I was a child, what did I daydream about?

When I was a child, who was that special adult I always felt great around?

When I was a child, did I like myself?

When I was a child, could I paint?

When I was a child, could I create worlds with my mind? If so, what were these worlds like?

When I was a child, what games did I like to play the most?

When I was a child, who held me when I was scared and told me it would be okay?

When I was a child, did I talk to God?

When I was a child, what did I think of this world?

When I was a child, was I afraid to grow up? If so, why?

When I was a child, did I like adults?

When I was a child, did I like other children?

When I was a child, did I play with imaginary friends?

When I was a child, did I believe in angels or fairies?

When I was a child, did I feel safe?

When I was a child, did I feel happy?

When I was a child, what was my favorite toy?

When I was a child, who was my best friend?

When I was a child, what frustrated me the most?

When I was a child, what did I believe was possible?

When I was a child, what was my favorite color?

When I was a child, what was my favorite time of year?

When I was a child, what was my favorite type of weather?

When I was a child, did I believe I was a good person?

When I was a child, did I feel different from everyone else?

When I was a child, did I feel special?

When I was a child, did I feel loved?

When I was a child, what pet did I most want to have?

When I was a child, did I like being alone?

When I was a child, what was my biggest fear?

When I was a child, what was my greatest dream?

When I was a child, did I believe in myself?

Who am I when I am happy?

Who am I when I am angry?

Who am I when I am sad?

Who am I when I have won?

Who am I when I have failed?

Who am I when I have hurt someone?

Who am I when I have helped someone?

Who am I when my heart is broken?

Who am I when I am in love?

Who am I today?

Who am I in this moment?

Who am I when I look into the mirror?

Who am I when no one is looking?

Who am I when I am in front of a crowd?

Who am I when I am with my friends?

Who am I when I am with my family?

Who am I when I am at my worst?

Who am I when my world crumbles?

Who am I when I am shining?

Who am I in the depths of my heart?

Who am I?

The subsequent follow-up questions are simply to help you process the exercise you just completed. As you read, you may write your answers down or simply answer them to yourself, whichever makes you feel most comfortable. Imagine that I am sitting across from you in a chair, listening to you as you share your answers to these questions.

How was that experience for you?

Did you like what you discovered?

Did some of it scare you?

Did some of it please you?

Were you able to answer the questions easily?

Did you find yourself really searching for answers?

Did your answers provide for you the ability to understand more fully who you are?

As you awaken to your authentic self, more and more will be revealed to you. In the meantime, please know that our world awaits the incredible arrival of YOU!

8 THE SPIRITUAL YOU

"Just as a candle cannot burn without fire, men cannot live without a spiritual life."

Buddha (563 – 483 B.C.)

With almost everyone I have worked with, I have found a simple common thread running through the healing process. This thread usually surfaces right around the same time with each client. It appears after they have actively done their inner work, are living each day from a new perspective of wholeness, and are witnessing great changes in their lives. However, in almost every case, my clients seem to hit a healing barrier or wall. They find themselves being and doing all the "right" things. Yet, they experience and feel that something is still missing. Time and time again, I have witnessed that when we work together to uncover the missing thread, it inevitably turns out to be directly related to their spiritual life.

I define spiritual life as the part of our lives that precisely relates to our belief system, connection, and relationship with our "spirit" or "soul" and a "Supreme Being." This Supreme Being comes in all forms depending upon one's religion or upbringing. In our American and global culture there are many names for this Supreme Being. Simply for the purpose of this writing, I will use the word *God.* In the monotheistic religions such as Judaism, Islam, and Christianity, *God* is believed to be the Supreme Being who is the All-Powerful, All-Knowing Creator of the Universe and all that exists in it. In polytheistic religions, there are several gods or spirits who rule and dictate the forces of the world.

Depending upon your upbringing, culture, religion, and own self-exploration, the word *God* will immediately elicit certain images, feelings, perceptions, and beliefs. I have often found, through my work, when someone has a negative response or feeling to the word or image of *God*, it is quite often related to "God" being seen as the "Judge, Jury, and Punisher." Many times, this perception leaves one with the belief that *God* is to be feared.

I have also found that even when the word or image of *God* feels positive and loving, when we dig deeply enough, there are still some remnants of a fear associated with *God.* This fear often turns out to be a fear of *God* not providing, *God* not taking care of, *God* not protecting, *God* not following through, or *God* not delivering what the person really needs. These fears, although they can be very subtle, are powerful. They are powerful because most of the time people are not aware of how these fears negatively affect their perceptions, thoughts, and realities in their daily life. For example, if a man is facing the loss of his income and he has a deeply-seated, subtle belief that *God* will not provide, this belief will then directly and negatively impact what he will experience with his current life circumstance. This negative impact then perpetuates the belief on an even deeper level and the cycle continues on and on.

The other major fear we find when we dig deeply into our spiritual self is the fear of being alone—a real and actual belief of being separate or separated from *God*. When people believe and fear that they are separate from *God*, their belief carries layers and layers of negative effects. They are often left feeling a void, loss, and emptiness—an internal disconnect. Many times, this disconnect is where the core root of addictive behaviors stem from. They begin "filling the void" inside with elements from the outside. Because they seek to gain a connection or to fill a void, they erroneously find solace in destructive and excessive behaviors, such as drugs, alcohol, food, sex, work, relationships, shopping, exercising, hoarding, and gambling. While these elements can all create an immediate "fix" or emotional bandage, eventually, such behaviors leave them in a worse off, more isolated and broken place than where they started. Though they might gain an immediate fix, their genuine need of healing and dissolving their fear of *God* is far from fulfilled.

Regardless of the origin of a fear of *God*, I have found that most any type of fear around or about *God* often leaves one feeling guilty, shameful, and/or worthless. To further explain, if someone believes that *God*, the One who created him or her, is to be feared on any level or feels separated from and alone, then he or she must not be worth that much. In other words, this fear ends up producing a sense of powerlessness and insignificance for a person on a very deep and often unconscious level.

To understand this further, let us go back to what you have learned about your inner child. Take that information and apply it here on a universal level. Imagine for a moment all of humanity as the wounded inner child and add to that picture *God* as the offensive, harmful, or unavailable parent. Can you see the depths and layers of damage and wounds caused by such a relationship?

If there is any part of you that believes your Creator is out to get you, will not provide and care for you, or is separate from you, then you may have some negative associations and effects that can wrongly determine your self-worth and value. If these feelings are true for you, then your belief ultimately will negatively affect all aspects of your life.

The underlying fear of *God* is what I have found to be the final wall or barrier to completing the healing process. If any fear of *God* exists, all the inner work—being consciously aware, acting as the objective observer of you, re-scripting negative or harmful thoughts, and inner child work—will only continue helping you to a certain extent. Ultimately, in order to successfully complete the healing process, all fear of *God*, no matter how grand or minute, must be removed from your beliefs.

But how? How do you remove this final block or hindrance to completing your healing process?

I believe the first step begins by looking at the semantics of this word *God*. The power a word has to elicit physical, emotional, or psychological response is amazing. For example, when you think of the word "lemon" what comes to mind? Is it a picture of a piece of fruit that is yellow in color, tart to the taste, and belonging to the citrus family? Now, what arises within you if you imagine that you have an open cut on your lip and you take a big bite out of a ripe, juicy lemon wedge? Did you feel any responses in your body, thoughts, or feelings? Let us try another example with the word "elevator." Notice what comes to mind for you. Do you picture a square box with doors, which slide open and close? Now, I want you to imagine yourself stepping into an elevator, pushing the 11th floor number, the doors closing, and feeling the elevator carry you to your desired floor location. When you think of this scene, can you feel the sensation of the elevator lifting up? Perhaps, if there is some fear around elevators, you may feel a bit of anxiety or discomfort. If you have no fear of elevators, you simply imagine the scene and remember what it is like to ascend.

A word's power is not based in the letters it is formed with, but rather your relationship, ideas, beliefs, images, and feelings about what the word symbolizes. The associations attached to a word are very subjective and unique to each person. One word can affect one person very strongly and have no effect on another at all.

If the actual word, thought, or image of *God* causes any negative, unloving, or fearful reactions within you, simply substitute the word *God* for a term with which you feel more comfortable. To help you do so, now is the time to bring out your personal notebook and explore what this word *God* means for you. Ask yourself, *What does the word God mean to me?* Then write or draw your answers out in your notebook. Explore where these thoughts, ideas, and feelings about *God* originated. Quiz yourself about each feeling, image, and thought that arises within you. Ask yourself, *Is this my true belief or did I learn this from someone*?

Once you have finished answering these questions, I encourage you to create or select a word, which symbolizes *God* for you. This word will be the right word for you if it provides positive, warm, and loving feelings for you. If you feel uncomfortable choosing a word or do not have one in mind, the following list of terms may be able to help you:

Love
Creator
The Holy One
The Holy Father
The Holy Mother
Source
Energy
Father/Mother God
Spirit
The Divine
Mommy-Poppy God
Jesus
Goddess
Buddha
The Holy Spirit
Hu
Mahatma
Supreme Being
Allah
The Alpha and Omega
Higher Power
Light and Love
Truth
Loving Mother
Loving Father
Yahweh
The One
The Big Guy
Divine Mother
Divine Father
The Big Dog
The I AM
Shiva
Ki
Chi
Prana
Qi
The Force
Universal Life Force
Energy
The Head of it All
The All in All
The Universe
… or even Fred.

Ultimately, the word, title, or phrase you use is not important. What is important is *your* comfort level with the word. Remember, the goal is to evoke and feel positive, warm, and loving feelings from the word, phrase, or term you choose. Whatever it is you choose, you want to experience a calming peaceful sense of a loving connection. It is important to remember that what we are really talking about here is not the actual word or words, but rather your feelings associated with the term or phrase you choose.

Once you have chosen your own special word to symbolize a name for your *God*, the next step has to do with understanding and developing your own personal relationship with your *God*. To help assist you with this, I would like for you to take out your personal notebook. On a new sheet of paper, draw a line down the middle of the page creating two columns. On the left column write the heading: *What I believe about God*. On the right column, write the heading: *What I want to believe or wish was true about God*. Please remember that for the purpose of this book, I am using the term *God*; just substitute your own chosen word whenever you see the word *God*. Now, in each of the columns, write down all of your thoughts and beliefs for each heading. In this exercise, freely write whatever comes to your mind. Do your best to completely fill in each column. Once you are finished with your writing, reread all that you have written. Now, to have a little fun with this, you get to be your own editor! Go through all you have written and cross out all you do not want to keep in your belief system any longer. Just cross it out with the mighty stroke of your pen. As you do this, say to yourself, *I freely let this old belief go…and so it is!* Once you have completed this part, you get to highlight and illuminate all you want to keep. In addition, if there were anything you would like to add, this is the time to do so. Add whatever your heart desires. As you add your newly inspired beliefs, make sure to reread every word and then ask yourself, *Do I like this*? If you do not, simply repeat these steps until you get to a place where you really like what you have created.

Once you feel really good about your answers, it is time to take the next step.

Simply re-write your newly desired image of *God* on a fresh sheet of paper. From this point on, reread this definition on a daily basis. As you continue on your healing path, use the above steps and amend it to your heart's content. Continue this daily exercise until you are completely satisfied and comfortable with your true definition of your personal identity and relationship with *God*.

The third step is to invite your new personal relationship with *God* into a conscious level. A good tool to use to accomplish this is your *white room*. This time, instead of it being the meeting place for your inner child, your white room will be the meeting place or sacred place for you and your *God*. As you performed in earlier exercises, you will be using your most vivid imagination in order to create your white room. Just as a reminder, the room you create in your mind is entirely white. The walls are white. The floors are white. The ceiling is white. This white room is absolutely perfect for you. Its size and shape are whatever will be most comfortable for you. It is big enough for you to feel open and free. It is small enough for you to feel safe, cozy, and protected. The room is uncluttered by any furniture or possessions. There are many large windows allowing a steady stream of beautiful golden-white light in to illuminate the room. The abundance of this light fills your white room with complete warmth, guidance, and Love. This room is a very special and unique place. It is always completely safe and a place where you are always protected, provided for, cared for, nurtured, and unconditionally loved in each and every moment. Your white room is entirely filled with the perfect amount of light and all the safety, comfort, care, nurturing, and Love *you individually* will ever need or desire. In your mind, you will bring to your awareness your personal white room and then simply enter into it. If you become stuck, just remember this is all in your imagination.

Now, feel, see, hear, or sense yourself as you enter the room. Simply experience yourself in this wonderful place. Embrace how this white room feels for you. Notice what your thoughts are, how your body feels, and how your emotions feel. Once you are fully experiencing your white room, it is time to intend to meet your personal *God*. Consciously choose to feel yourself opening up to this experience. Allow yourself to experience this exercise with simple ease and grace. From this point, simply and warmly say aloud, *Hello.* Then, just be still and present in the moment. Allow whatever your experience is meant to be, to simply be. You can repeat this step as many times as you need. Simply allow your experience to be uniquely yours.

Once you get past the initial *Hello*, you can use the white room as a tool to continue exploring and deepening your personal relationship with your *God*. In addition, you can journal in your personal notebook any questions, ideas, and thoughts that arise for you along the way. Then, when you use your white room, simply bring these specific aspects to your experience and ask for clarity, guidance, and understanding. The goal here is to bring your personal relationship with your *God* to a deeper and more profound level.

As with any full and rich relationship, your healthy spiritual relationship will need your time and devotion. The amount of your personal time and devotion is completely in your hands. Your spiritual relationship with your *God* is defined by you and you alone. What a fantastic relationship in which to grow in and share with the world!

I have consciously written this book so that you may feel as if I am right there with you, sharing with you, listening to you, and providing tools, which help to guide your healing process along the way. My intention has been to encourage, support, and honor your own unique inner journey. I would like to continue with that journey from a more personal place. The following information is simply my truth, which I have discovered on my own journey. I am sharing this with you so that it may offer something personal for you. If what I share feels right for you, please keep it; if it does not, please leave it. Take only what feels helpful and nurturing for you and your path.

From the time I was a child, I felt a deeply profound connection and closeness to *God*. I spouted knowledge of *God* to my parents, friends, family, and pretty much anyone who would listen. I felt such a strong responsibility to tell, teach, and guide everyone I could back to *God*. From the time I could process thought, I knew I was born to do this work and so I have, but not without my own learning. You see, through the bumps and bruises, the trials and errors, the successes and failures along the course of my life, I have come to realize the greatest understanding about my purpose:

I cannot teach what is already known. I cannot give someone something they inherently already possess.

My purpose now is to live what I know and share with and inspire those who ask.

Therefore, please know I am not here to tell you what your relationship with *God* is to be, should be, needs to be, or shall be. I believe that there is neither person nor religion nor philosophy that can tell you or anyone what their relationship is with *God*. I feel each of us has our own unique relationship with The Divine. I have come to understand that we all have a blueprint to our own spiritual relationship. This blueprint is located within each of us, within our own hearts. Sure, we can be inspired, explore, learn, grow, and expand in our knowledge of *God*, but ultimately, our own heart is the actual doorway. Our heart is the very portal to a personal relationship and connection with *God*. Our heart has the ability to transcend all fear and error and deliver us straight to *God*. I truly believe our heart is the gateway to LOVE. All we have to do is consciously ask to have our heart open up and reveal to us our path, truth, and understanding.

You are a miraculous and wondrous being. You were created in Love and are sustained in Love. Everything you need is within you, for that is where God is.

These words were given to me by *God* when my daughter was born. I repeated them to her every day of her infancy, toddler years, and early childhood. After that, she would tell me, "I know, Mama. You don't have to tell me anymore."

How beautiful!

How beautiful it is to know so deeply the truth of these words.

Is there a greater gift any of us can have?

God is Love. I am not talking about the false, romanticized, Hollywood-version of love, but rather, the Principle of Love.

I believe *God* is Love and the Source from which all of us—you and I—were created.

From the point of our creation, through all of eternity—then, now, and forever—we remain One with *God*.

God has never left us. We have never really left *God*.

Just as a thought can never leave its thinker, we can never truly leave *God*. As a ray from the sun extends from its source, so we extend from *God*. Sometimes, I know it can seem and feel that we are lost and disconnected from Love—especially on those days where it appears nothing is going right or during those periods in our lives when our troubles feel so heavy we wonder if they will ever end. No matter the time or circumstance, we are never alone. *God* is always with us.

We are never alone.

We are always One with *God*.

God is always One with us.

I believe we are co-creators with *God*.

Every day, we have the amazing gift and opportunity to design our lives together. We have the chance to create masterpieces with the Most High.

Our lives are not meant to be about pain, suffering, sacrifice, misery, torture, paying a price, or paying off a debt. These dynamics are from the old paradigm, which did not serve us well and are no longer necessary. Now, our lives are to be about living!

Real living

Living in the moment

Moment to moment with

Love, Joy, and Creation from our

Highest Place of Being

Experiencing in all of it...

Delight.

Laughter.

Creativity.

Expansion.

Enjoyment.

...and breathing it all in, every step of the way.

I believe we were created to live happily and extend that happiness outwardly expanding ourselves, one another, and the Universe through a beautiful, joyful co-creation of existence. I believe we are meant to positively influence this world and Universe.

We are meant to live in Joy with a full and expanding heart. We are meant to play.

Dance.

Sing.

Frolic.

Laugh.

Love!

As we expand ourselves with Joy, *God* celebrates with us and through us. *God* desires our most Perfect Happiness. I believe that when we are happy and live from a place of spiritual richness, we not only thrive and flourish—we actually help heal the world with each and every moment of our experience.

These are the truths I have come to understand from my inner journey. I encourage you to ask yourself: "What are my truths? What would I like to believe? How do I want my spiritual life to be expressed in my life?"

As you keep asking, searching, and discovering your truth, your journey truly becomes yours.

9

CONTINUING YOUR JOURNEY

"The only journey is the one within."

Rainer Maria Rilke, Austrian-German poet and author (1875 – 1926)

As our time here together in this book comes to a close, I would like to provide some further guidance for continuing your journey. Through your reading and active participation in the exercises, you have had the opportunity to grow, expand, learn, understand, increase your awareness, and shift in great ways. This book is meant to be read and reread. Each time you read it and actively participate in the exercises, you will have further opportunity to obtain more awareness and gain a deeper and more profound understanding. In addition, as you continue to use your personal notebook, it will become a tool of personal measurement. You will be able to use it to look back over and witness with your own eyes your amazing process. Therefore, let us go ahead and place this book, its exercises, and your personal notebook in your toolbox.

Now, let us take a long look at how full your toolbox is:

1. Taking Full Responsibility for Yourself and Your Life
2. Being Consciously Aware and Acting as the Objective Observer of You
3. Identifying, Removing, and Re-scripting Your Thoughts
4. Meeting and Healing Your Inner Child
5. Gaining an Awareness of each Gender's Desires in a Relationship
6. Learning Effective Communication Skills: Clarity, Style of Delivery, and Active Listening Skills
7. Being and Living from Your Authentic Self
8. Connecting with and developing Your Spiritual Life

As you continue on your journey, you will come across other tools you will be able to include in your toolbox to help guide you along your way. The following reading list is a mere start to finding other tools for your journey:

The Hidden Messages in Water *by Masaru Emoto*

The Alchemist *by Paulo Coelho*

The Five Love Languages *by Gary Chapman*

Jonathan Livingston Seagull *by Richard Bach*

There's No Such Place As Far Away *by Richard Bach*

Ask and It Is Given *by Esther and Jerry Hicks*

The Twelve Gifts of Birth *by Charlene Costanzo*

A Return to Love *by Marianne Williamson*

A Course in Miracles *by Foundation for Inner Peace*

The Biology of Belief *by Bruce Lipton*

Your favorite Poetry

Your favorite Literature

In addition to further reading to discover new tools for your toolbox, I have found the following tools to be valuable as well...

Witnessing nature

Connecting with nature

"Being" with nature

Witnessing art that moves you

Connecting with art

Creating your own art

Witnessing music that stirs you

Connecting with music

Creating your own music

Allowing yourself to walk in the rain

Expressing yourself in song

Doing anything you were always afraid to do

Forgiving

Letting go

Being in the present moment

Breathing one breath at a time

Loving unconditionally!

As you continue on your personal journey and stay open and receptive, your inner guidance will lead you to your next steps and tools, which are perfect for you.

In the beginning of this book I asked, *If you could look in the mirror right now, what type of painting would you see? What does your self-portrait look like? What colors, shades, and hues show up, and what do they represent in your painting? What types of textures, light effects, and brush strokes make up your painting?* As your process continues, simply add the new colors, shapes, textures, and brush strokes you like. Create your portrait so it reflects all that you are—the uniquely magnificent you. You have the opportunity right now to *be* the masterpiece your truly are!

On this wonderful path of self-discovery, you have opened amazing doors of healing for yourself and your relationships. All you have to do now is keep going. Continue on each day with all you now know and allow yourself to experience everything more you will discover. Make the absolute commitment to yourself to continue the healing journey for You. Your healing process is your gift to yourself and all those around you. When you take each healing step and commit to the process, you positively affect yourself, your partner, your children, your family, your friends, your community, everyone your life touches, generations to come, and our world!

I want to congratulate you on coming this far and offer you the greatest encouragement for you to keep going! Take this place where you have found yourself and use it as your springboard into all that is You.

Our world and everyone in it is blessed when you truly are the masterpiece you were created to be!

I wish for you Abundant Blessings and the Fulfillment of All Your Heart's Desires.

In Gratitude and With Much Love,

Bree

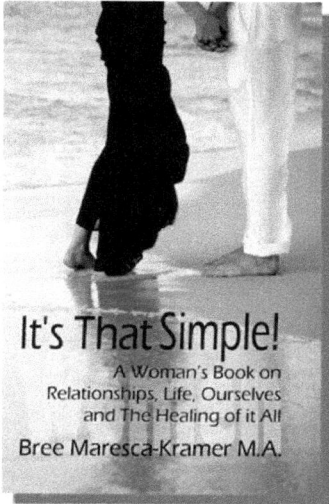

www.ingramcontent.com/pod-product-compliance
Lightning Source LLC
Chambersburg PA
CBHW060847280326
41934CB00007B/953
* 9 7 8 1 9 3 5 6 5 8 0 1 6 *